HUNTED IN THE WOODS

Sometimes predators are animal or human

....and sometimes they are not.

Stephen Young

Copyright © 2015 by Stephen Young.

All rights reserved.

Table of Contents

Introduction 1

Chapter 1: The Chitauli, Hunting humans, and Body drops. 5

Chapter 2: Magickal Working, Art, and Ancient Races 46

Chapter 3: Caves, Caverns, and Screams 77

Chapter 4: Silence & Blood-curdling Screams in the woods 96

Chapter 5: Non-humans in the woods 109

Chapter 6: A case like Dyatlov 123

Chapter 7: Hunted by Humans? 136

Chapter 8: Taken, Held, and Drowned 151

Chapter 9: Shape-Shifters & Missing Time 207

Conclusion 214

Excerpts from Mysterious things in the Woods 215

Excerpts from Predators in the Woods 224

Excerpts from Something in the Woods is Taking People 231

Introduction

Following on from the bestselling book series 'Something in The Woods is Taking People,' as featured on Coast to Coast AM.

The mysterious disappearances of people, both adults and children, have taken place around the world since antiquity, leaving no tracks, trails, or any possible evidence as to what might have happened to them, and so often, the missing are never found; or, they are returned in a very different condition to when they disappeared..

Thoughts, ideas, and theories about each individual case of 'the disappeared,' and the causes of each of these disappearances are often well documented and discussed ad infintum, and yet overwhelmingly, what they lack in each case are accurate conclusions and definitive proof about what really happened to the missing, and often this is never discovered, despite the comprehensive and exhaustive involvement of law enforcement agencies, the military, expert searchers and trackers, and hundreds of volunteers.

Other cases seem to slip by with far less attention and investigation, and yet they display the same mysterious and often inexplicable characteristics of a person anomalously disappearing.

What really lies behind these many mysterious disappearances? What is the real reason for the ones who are returned either dead, or returned but changed, never to be the same again?

This book deals with some documented cases, many previously unknown, and takes a deep look into what are some of the most compelling, perplexing, and disturbing cases of strange and unexplained disappearances of people across the world. Some of the evidence uncovered is both surprising and shocking. Some of the possible causes are both terrifying and horrific. Some of the possible answers are ones that we probably don't want to believe....because that would change the entire way we view our world and force us to reconsider who the predators really are.

In a famous interview with John Keel in 1973, called 'The Great UFO Wave,' by Glenn Wayne and David Graham, Keel made some interesting comments,

"On the ground, and air, there are things happening that they don't want us to know about. What they are trying to hide may be frightening, even incomprehensible, but it does seem they are using us."

He then makes a very shocking statement. "It may be more than rumor that young people are being 'collected' from colleges after the memories of their families and friends have been altered so that they will not remember the existence of their children. As farfetched as this sounds, there may be more truth to it than to some of the other theories kicked around."

Unbelievable as it may sound, he is saying explicitly that he believes college kids are being permanently abducted and not returned. Not only that, but he says their families are being tampered with too.

"We are being used in some fashion,' he says, just as his predecessor Charles Fort once said, "We are being fished," and, Keel continues, "intelligences" don't want us to discover how they are using us... so, all this other stuff is camouflage."

This 'other stuff' he refers to, is the manifestation of strange and anomalous sightings of entities which appear to defy both categorisation and explanation.

"(We) have been misled for years by deliberately misleading manifestations and chimeras, (which) range from complex hallucinations, to elaborate transmogrifications."

Both Keel and Charles Fort then, sincerely believed that there were people going missing...who never came back, or came back changed, and diversion tactics are put in place to conceal this.

As wild as this sounds, some of the cases that follow appear not only to sound just as unbelievable and far-fetched; but equally, they also appear to back-up what both men believed, and horrifically, they're cases that really happened.

Sometimes predators are human or animal....and sometimes they are not.

This book deals with the stuff of nightmares. It revolves around allegations of the most horrific kind, involving missing children, non-human predators, patsies, and assassinations. Could any of it really be true? Here is a presentation of the twists and turns of a stream of allegations and supposed revelations to horrify anyone reading it.

Chapter 1:
The Chitauli, Hunting humans, and Body drops

Credo Mutwa is an internationally known Zulu shaman and healer. He gave a startling interview to Rick Martin of the Spectrum Newspaper back in 1999. What he said, is a terrifying revelation, if it could possibly be true.

"Over 1,000 children disappear in South Africa every month. The Newspapers say it is organised child prostitution, but I don't think so. These children are not street children; they are school children who stand out in class, because they are good at subjects."

"When shamans in Zaire talk of 'the Lords who control Earth,' they are the Chitauli's, although there are 24 other alien races we know of. The field Chitauli's eyes glow red. They are tall with large heads. They walk gracefully. Some have horns around their heads; these are the warriors. The royals have no horns. They have a claw which is very sharp and straight, which they use to punch into the human nose in order to drink human brains in their ritual."

"If they are sick, a young girl is kidnapped by the servants and taken to the underground. There the girl is bound and forced to lie next to the sick one for weeks, being fed and cared for, but kept tied. Once the sick one is well, the girl is given a chance to escape, *a chance which it isn't*, for when the girl escapes she is chased over a long distance underground by flying creatures made of metal, and captured when she reaches the peak of fear and exhaustion."

"Then she is taken to an altar and sacrificed, and her blood drunk. The victim must not be sacrificed until she is very frightened. This chasing was practiced by Zulu cannibals; their descendants will tell you that the flesh of the human being who was made to run to try and escape and has been very frightened, tastes better than the flesh of a person who was simply killed."

"Here, and it is still ongoing, five white girls disappeared. Each one was a highly talented child, either developing in spiritual ability, or a leader in school subjects. It was a big story in the News and people came to me and persuaded me to try and find these children. Then my phone started ringing and with very angry voices, I was told to stop helping. 'They' told me that if I didn't stop, my children would be murdered. Sure enough, my youngest was brutally stabbed, and so I stopped."

"After the disappearance of the children, the police arrested a reverend called Reverend Van Rooyen and his girlfriend. Before he appeared in court, a very strange thing happened. They were shot in their vehicle. After they were shot, their vehicle managed to come to a stop; something a moving truck would never do."

"They had been murdered. Why do I say that? Because he had a gunshot wound in his right temple, and yet, all who knew him said he was left-handed man. So, who murdered them? It is one of the ugliest mysteries."

It should be pointed out here that the Newspapers of the time have a different version; they say that the man's girlfriend lured the children away, the children were spotted in the man's company, and that it was the Reverend who sexually assaulted then murdered them. Their bodies however have never been found to confirm this belief, though the police didn't doubt he was their suspect. Credo's belief however is that they were not the right suspects; that the suspects were not even human.

"I can't help but wonder if the Chitauli are in the U.S. because of the large number of underground bases. The number of missing children in the U.S. alone is so astronomically high that the slave trade does not answer the question."

At the time of giving this interview, Credo said that he was visited by three people who told him to stop talking or his wife would die.

Could this really be what happened? Is there really a blood-drinking reptilian race of beings, who take pleasure in hunting humans? While many will say his account is pure fable, thousands around the world believe what he says and he is highly respected for his nature and conservation work and recognised as one of the most distinguished healers internationally.

A few years ago, another man came out with claims just as horrific. Investigative conspiracy researcher Dave Starbuck, now in his 70's, has been producing DVD's of highly controversial conspiracy related topics for decades in the U.K. (his website is revelationaudiovisual.com)

In 2006, he interviewed a man called Dean Warwick. Dean claimed he was a civil engineer who worked on bridge and tunnel projects for the US government in the mid '60's. He described himself as a "whistleblower." He was also an 'alternative energy' pioneer and claimed to be "an insider within US intelligence." He also claimed to be ex-British intelligence.

Originally from New Zealand, he said his Grandfather worked in the justice department and was a high level Mason. Warwick said his grandfather was also a world renown expert in 'Chinese detection.' In Chinese, 'detection' means the inspection of an 'object' which can't be observed; and in Warwick's case, he meant the detection of 'people,' picked out and stalked without them knowing it; in other words, putting a tail on someone.

Warwick says that when his Grandfather was on his deathbed, "he told me something as he was dying; he said that later on in life I would learn something which he couldn't divulge to me. I was 15 at the time. He said it was something that would practically destroy me, and I'm quite convinced that I do know now what it is that he was talking about, and it is truly horrifying."

"It is not being made public; I have yet to see, read or hear anywhere of evidence of that which I have learned, and I have many confirming reports from police around the U.K. and from Church groups that I was mixed with in the U.S. before coming to the U.K."

"I was drafted into the New Zealand Army, and topped every course in the officers training while preparing for Vietnam. I was taught how to bring down the Twin Towers using nothing but infrasound; we were made to study the experts; the Russians, the Americans, and the British in the late '50's. When I was in the military, there were these joint manoeuvres in the late 50's by these Superpowers, bringing down tower blocks using nothing but sound waves. Later, I became a civil and structural engineer."

"Now back to what I mentioned earlier; it's to do with the killing of the children. We have got a release from the US department of statistics in which it's said that every year, there will be 150,000 children disappear and never be heard of again. A similar report said in Central and S. America there will be 350,000. That's .5% of the population of N. America; and .5 % of Southern and Central America. Exactly the same figure; that can't be a coincidence. Then one day I've got a suit walks into my office and we get talking and he says he has a meeting at the department for social security, work and pensions.

So I tell him, "Have a look at something; I think you'll be interested," and as he looks at the reports I say, "We don't have anything like that in the U.K."

He replies, "I will tell you who I am; I'm head of that department, I've been there more than 3 decades. There's 20 to 25,000 children a year disappearing in the UK."

Warwick continues, "*The Mothers of the Disappeared* group says that each year in the UK, 120,000 children disappear, and 20% will never be found again. That's the same figure this man walked in and told me. So what's happening to these kids?" he asks rhetorically; and here is where it gets truly horrific, if it's at all possible that it could really be true.

He says, "I have it from an officer in the police in a southern police force; each week they find up to 7 or 8 children in the New Forest that have been slit around their necks and down their shoulders; their skin has been peeled off their backs and their flesh has been eaten while they are alive."

He continues, "And this brings me to the Jessica & Holly case."

(Here he is referring to the murders of Jessica Chapman and Holly Wells. In August of 2002, the two young best friends, aged just ten years old, and probably best remembered for the photo taken of them wearing their Manchester United football T-shirts, went missing after going out to buy some sweets after dinner.

When they didn't return home, their families tried to reach them on Jessica's mobile phone but they couldn't get her to pick up. Holly didn't have a phone. By midnight, the police were out searching for them in the small Cambridgeshire village of Soham. Volunteers joined them and they searched all night, the next day, and for the entire week.

During that week, many witnesses came forward to say they had seen the two children that evening when they had gone to buy the sweets, and one of these witnesses was a Senior School caretaker, Ian Huntley, who lived with the girls' Primary School teacher, Maxine

Carr. He said that he had seen the two children that evening when they had walked by his house.

When the police talked to him about the children, they found his behaviour unusually 'emotional' and it aroused their suspicions when he kept asking them lots of questions. As the days passed by, he seemed to be maintaining a high visibility in the search process and with the visiting media too, and subsequently, a few days later, they returned to his house and searched it, but found nothing there that would indicate he had anything to do with the children disappearing.

In the second search of the School where he worked however, they found the half-burnt football T-shirts the girls had been wearing, and he was arrested for their murders. It was 13 days after the girls went missing that their charred bodies were found in a ditch in the woods near the US Air Force base Lakenheath, in Suffolk, discovered by a man who kept pheasants in the area. It was a thirty minute drive away from the village they lived in.

Forensic evidence of fibres matching the girls' clothes was found in the suspect's car and house, as well as his hairs on their T-shirts and fibres from his clothes.

He was sent to trial and found guilty of double murder and sentenced to life in prison.

Shockingly however, according to Warwick, "Anybody who believes that Ian Huntley had anything to do with it needs their head examined."

His interviewer, Dave Starbuck concurs. "I agree; I did a presentation about it and the response was so tremendous, including from two Solicitors and a Barrister," he says.

Why would these two avid researchers make such a claim? Well, it appears that it has to do with what Warwick said earlier, about the claims he makes about bodies being found in the New Forest, and about how he believes the two children in this case really died. As wild and outrageous as it sounds, Warwick, (now deceased, and this I will come to later) insists that the murderer Huntley was a 'patsy,' to cover up the real cause of these children's deaths. It has to be said that his belief, which he says has been corroborated, makes for very insensitive reading when it concerns the real deaths of these two children, and for the parents of the two children, it seems wrong for Warwick to makes such allegations when it would be highly distressing to them.

However, in his words, he says, "What we have is he was there (in the woods where the girls were found) because they found seeds in his trousers from the plants there. (But) He could have got them from anywhere *or*, they could have been planted."

In other words, what he means is that for the Crown Prosecution, the existence of the seeds gave them clear evidence that the man was there and dumped the bodies there because of the seeds found in his trousers; what Warwick is suggesting however, is that they could have been planted on him to enable his prosecution, by deliberately placing him at the scene, when in fact Warwick clearly believes he wasn't at the scene and the evidence was tampered with.

He continues, "So, he takes their bodies to the woods, takes off their clothes, and pours petrol on their bodies. No! You would leave the clothes on to soak up the petrol and make the fire burn better. Then, he takes the clothes back to his school, finds a bin and puts the clothes inside of it, and pours some petrol on them and sets them on fire. Nonsense!"

Again, what he is saying is, why would he burn the bodies in a remote part of the woods miles away, to try to hide them and destroy the evidence, but then take their clothes to his place of work to burn, thereby risking a far higher chance of the remains of the clothes being found where he works and obviously certainly implicating himself; which he did when they were then found by the police. Also, how were hairs found on the T-shirts yet the T-shirts had been burnt?

And now here come the chilling parts alleged;

Warwick says, "We have the lady who tried to get a newspaper to print her story. Whether it's true or not I don't know but she says she walked her dog in that wood *every day* for two weeks before their bodies were found. She said that the military police were there then and they were blocking off the path."

His interviewer Starbuck adds, "Correct; I heard that from another source."

Warwick continues, "We have the jogger interviewed outside the court as the trial was ongoing. He said that *for three nights* he had been running in those woods and he had heard girls screaming. My information comes from high level US intelligence. Those girls bodies were treated with a set of talons and they were raped. Now whether this was part of a cult or it is a part of a 'transmutation' of a presence is open to argument."

This sounds utterly horrifying, but utterly insane. Surely this is crazy? Isn't it very bad taste to even suggest that these girls suffered an even more horrific fate than at the hands of a child predator of human origin? What he is saying is that they were attacked and killed by 'entities' with talons, as with the other cases, and "their skin peeled off and their flesh eaten while they are alive," and the 'murderer' used as a 'patsy,' to cover it up.

However, if we look closer at the murderer, he would appear to be the perfect candidate to commit these killings. He would appear to completely fit the perfect profile of a human predator. It seems that he was known to the police for a while before he was arrested for these murders. He'd been investigated in 1995 for having relations with an underage girl. He was arrested for house burglary that year too but the charges were ordered to lie on file rather than convict him. Why was that? He is accused again of having underage sex. Then the following year another 15 year old alleges he is having relations with her, but her family decide not to take further action.

The following month the police and social service investigate him for allegations he is having sex with a 13 year old. The girl refuses to co-operate. A month later he is arrested when a woman says he raped her after they shared a taxi home from a nightclub. The police say there is insufficient evidence. A month later he is arrested for rape of a woman walking home alone from a nightclub. The crown prosecution decide the CCTV footage is insufficient and there is insufficient evidence to charge him. Two months later, a 12 year old girl alleges he sexually assaulted her. Again, the police decide there is not enough evidence, despite her detailed testimony. In February 1999, a 17 year old girl tells the police that he raped her. He says it was consensual. The police drop the case.

Of course, those who believe Warwick's version that it was not a human who did this but entities with talons, will say that these arrests and charges against Huntley make him the perfect candidate to choose as a patsy. He fits the perfect profile of a serial sexual predator, whose behaviour has then escalated to murder. He couldn't really be a better candidate for the prosecution to get their hands on.

While the idea that he was a patsy sounds completely outlandish when aligned with the claims Warwick makes of 'reptilian' entities skinning children alive; it does arouse suspicion because he was never convicted of any of his offences, and it has to be asked why a man accused by multiple girls and young women of very serious assaults was never, in all of those cases, even once taken to trial and convicted of them. This would certainly add fuel to Warwick's belief that Huntley was the perfect patsy to be used; it was almost as though he was 'allowed' to get off with these charges as part of a pre-planned cover-up of the 'reptilian' child killings; that, or he was 'selected' as the perfect candidate from the criminal database.

On the other hand, a more sensible explanation probably lies in the fact that its really not uncommon for Social Services to fail vulnerable children who complain of assault; there are cases repeatedly in the News where the 'system' has failed to safeguard them, and its also common for the police and crown prosecution to fail victims of sexual assault. It also seems that in this case, there was also a failure too of liaison between different organisations and departments, and there was also the fact that when he applied for the role of caretaker at the school, he used a different surname. This meant that his robbery charge did not flag up.

Of course, none of his sexual assaults showed up either because the police and crown prosecution service said there was 'insufficient evidence' in every case. The headmaster of the school had no idea of the real background of Huntley, and different jurisdictions and departments seemed to fail to notice that he was repeatedly flagging up as a perpetrator of serious assaults. With the repeated complaints against him, and lack of any convictions, it certainly adds fuel to the conspiracy theory that he actually didn't do it. However, the alternative explanation is far too crazy and horrifying to believe, surely?

Another argument against Warwick's case of the 'skinning alive' non-human predators, is that of the Australian investigative journalist & conspiracy theorist Joe Viallis (now deceased) who also put forwards the theory that Ian Huntley was a patsy, but for an entirely different reason. He says that just metres away (although it was more like half a mile) from where the bodies of the girls were found is LakenHeath US Air Force base. Viallis' reason for Huntley being the patsy in this case was, he alleges, to cover up the real perpetrator of the murders of the girls, because, he believes, he was a US military man and it was done for diplomatic reasons to ensure the Air Force base kept a sterling reputation and could maintain its good relationship with the people of the UK, however closer inspection in this shows that there is no obvious proof, but it does perhaps add to the belief of some people that Huntley was set up. While there are those who believe he was, the overwhelming majority of the public however simply do not believe he is innocent.

Another controversial researcher, David Dixon however, claims that a man and a woman had been seen before the children disappeared, staring at them intensely from a car, as though following them, and that a woman had tried to abduct a child nearby recently from a school. There are reams of information carried out by independent researchers who have looked into the myriad of discrepancies in this case, however, it's not the intention of this book to go off topic and look into that, and he certainly appears to have been a monster.

Returning instead to Warwick's revelations about the Huntley case and how it ties in with non-human predators, he doesn't stop there. His theory and alleged evidence gets even wilder. He refers to the Bible. In particular, he says, "A piece which recurs many, many times; 'And they ate the flesh of children in those days.'

There is a reason it says that. A client of mine is a scientist high up in British government research. In the Bible and much of what Zecharia Sitchin has written, is the story of how the Nephilim or Anunnaki ate the menstrual fluid of woman because from it, they derived the ability to read the mind of a person."

Surely this is unbelievable? He then goes on to explain that when these giants came down to earth and mated with human women, the women often died in childbirth, leaving them without women from which to 'eat' the ingredients he mentioned. As a replacement of this, (and while not addressing why they didn't just abduct more women) he then argues that instead they switched to something else, "The Nephilim or Anunnaki discovered that if a terrorized human child's flesh was eaten; and this I have (corroborated) from this scientific base, but I won't say where in the U.K; if that flesh is eaten, it's full of serotonin and adrenaline and it gives them these similar ingredients, which allows them to read minds."

"There are so many references to it in the Bible; it doesn't say they ate the bones, it doesn't say they ate the skin of children; it says 'ate the flesh' and that means that they had been skinned."

"I have this confirmed by police. And, the guillotines, as quoted in Revelations, are appearing. Thousands brought into military bases. What for? How are you going to 'reduce the population by 6 billion?!

Okay we can play games with the weather, we can cause floods. An English doctor and his family were walking in a Canadian forest near the American border and came to a disused rail yard with box cars and inside of them were shackles with a guillotine. Just consider that we are shackled and are left pointed at the guillotine and left waiting to be put into it until the next day; You're going to be terrified!" So here we get the adrenalin running!"

"The majority of people will say this is nonsense," he rightly says, but he points out that he believes it's because it's too big a thing for most people to even contemplate. Or, is it indeed nonsense and just the product of a wild imagination and too much reading? His claims are outlandish in the extreme, but then, even a cursory look on YouTube and you will find these alleged box cars and the stacks of empty coffins lined up in various parts of the US.

Has this man drunk too much conspiracy fuel? Or cobbled together a sci-fi story and is putting it around as some kind of factual existence? Of course, having no named sources does not help his argument at all. The New Forest is not a vast dense forest like a National Park in the US. Is it at all within the realms of possibility that something so extreme as the killing, skinning and eating of 7 to 8 children a week by the Anunnaki could be happening without people knowing? It sounds the most preposterous thing to suggest, and why would a policeman who is on the verge of suicide from witnessing the remains of the children not come forward and speak out against such things? His source, "this police officer, tells me that one of his colleagues is the one who has to inspect the bodies, and each time he is nearly suicidal from what he finds."

If this is the case, why doesn't he, or any of the other alleged witnesses or sources this man claims to have speak out too? On the other hand, what does happen to all the missing children he refers to from the official statistics? And, there's also the allegations that this man himself suffered a very drastic consequence as a result of speaking out.

The idea that he was onto something has grown somewhat in conspiracy circles, because of his rather sudden and possibly strange death, which occurred shortly after he came out with these allegations in the above interview. His supporters say he was killed. It happened, it's alleged, at a UFO conference in 2006, in Blackpool, England. He was giving a presentation there and was the last guest to go on stage. He had told his supporters and friends before the conference that he was going to blow the whistle on some highly controversial topics; missing children, ET's, NSA, the 9/11 attacks, and apparently he was even going to name 'the anti-christ.'

Just minutes into his talk however, he collapsed in front of the audience. He died there and then. The general consensus among his supporters is that he was hit by an ELF weapon. On the other hand, he was not a young man and could just as easily have had a genuine heart attack. One source quotes him as having heart problems but refusing to go to the Doctor, and laying a concrete path shortly before the conference, which perhaps might have extenuated his existing medical condition if that is what he did.

While some who attended the conference make claims of having seen a smartly dressed man leave the audience moments after the speaker collapsed, go down the stairs and exit the building merrily whistling, and making a telephone call on his mobile phone in which he was laughing heartily, having just seen the man collapse, Warwick's wife however told the New Zealand Newspaper's that she was satisfied her husband died of natural causes.

Whichever the case, we will probably never know; however, the things he came out with are certainly disturbing.

Another mysterious case comes from the 1970's, however in this case; it appears to be the unfortunate product of an over-active imagination and some embellishment. Or does it?

In 2008, 'The Watcher,' began posting on the Project Avalon forum. He appears to go by the name of Paul Grant, also nee Barry King. He says that the well known writer Andrew Collins wrote of the events in his life in a special report in 1978, but this has not been confirmed.

Part of his story revolves around an intriguing and highly sinister case, and appears to be backed up by now declassified letters sent to the Ministry of Defence. However, the real scenario will later turn out to be most likely wholly different.

Paul writes, "In 1970, my research centred on reports of sightings of lights and craft entering the King George reservoir, (in Waltham Forest, Enfield, England.) In March of 1970, two young children went missing in the area, and searches included the reservoir."

"Three months later, their bodies were found in a copse there. Great mystery surrounds their deaths. A press blackout ensued. The families were told not to speak with anyone. Strangely, the official word was that, even though summer, they died from exposure."

"I went to the scene myself and it did look very strange. The Police were in plain clothes, and the stranger part; the army were there too. The public were standing nearby, held back by police. No one knew what was going on. The Army were carrying spades and sacks. They removed the soil. Years later the grass still hardly grew there. The official version was that the children died of exposure, in summer, even though they were less than 500 metres from a street and houses."

"I trod on toes trying to get hold of information. A few months later, over several nights, two people were sitting in a car looking toward my house. Then saw my first run-in with MIB's; these were black-suited and of the NSA variety. The non-human ones came later."

Of the non-human MIB's he claims to have encountered, he says, "Most people will scoff; but many have come under their attention. They're menacing only if you show them fear; if you stand up to them and don't appear disturbed by their appearance, it's like a process kicks in as though they're not programmed for that response and they 'shut down.' If fear and stress is shown when under their attention, their pre-set programming of intimidation will continue."

His story about the missing children appears to be backed up by a 'persistent correspondent,' according to documents released by the Ministry of Defence, and now in Archives. Indicated on the files by the Ministry as 'closed,' yet according to the pen marks on the document it is labelled for "permanent retention."

The correspondence deals with a matter that according to the writer of the letters, is a very serious issue, and one that would certainly require attention in his opinion. It involves the account of the abduction and deaths of two children, caused allegedly, according to the UFO researcher, by aliens.

The researcher in question released a document called 'Age of Enigma,' from the West Country Unidentified Flying Object Research Association,' in March 2002.

In March 2011, the U.K. Department of Defence released UFO related correspondence it had received from members of the public, and the author of 'Age of Enigma,' had written to them concerning this case. The researcher from the UFO group (name redacted but presumably Paul Grant nee Barry King) says that he was an active researcher in this field after he had a sighting of his own, back in 1970. He subsequently joined the British UFO Research Association, or B.U.F.O.R.A.

The 'Age of Enigma; West Country Unidentified Flying Object Research Association report of March 2002, sent to the MOD reads, '"REDACTION ON ORIGINAL DOCUMENT"

'Myself and (Name redacted) left the pub in The Ridgeway, in Chingford, North London, at about 10.40 pm, Tuesday before Christmas, December 1970. When

I reached home I decided to walk along the line of shops close by. There were some people still out by the fish n chip shop. I continued on, then stopped and looked towards the top of the bank of the King George V reservoir when I saw two white horizontal round objects attached to a cable ascending the reservoir at 200 yards distance. There was no noise emitting from it. Then it descended, then veered upwards at a speed, then down, the cable still attached to it.'

'I stood for a minute or so before running back to the fish shop and said, "Quick, you must see this. A U.F.O. has landed!" We all ran back. After a period of about 45 minutes, the two silent objects descended inside the retaining bank.'

'Looking back now, I think it was a form of scanner. For some time after I was wondering about it, what had happened, but it wasn't until 18 months later that there was the strange disappearance of two children. They lived nearby. They turned up dead in a clump of trees, northeast of the reservoir. Police had gone all over with tracker dogs. It's strange they should disappear then reappear next to trees which had been burned from above. The local press printed that they died from bum marks and that they died from over exposure.'

(The first point regarding burn marks, I have not been able to corroborate)

The report continues, 'Their bodies were not found close together, and one of the girl's shoes was missing. The other shoe she was wearing was clean. If you drop two stones from the air they will not land in the same place or spot. Their bodies were not found together.'

'UFO's have been known to leave bum marks, they have been known to kill animals. The sun could not have caused the burns, just as it's unlikely that the children die from exposure- in June. I strongly believe that they came into contact with aliens. I feel they died under duress at the time of a U.F.O. flap.'

'When they were found and we arrived there, there were crowds of people and the police were everywhere, and the Ministry of Defence.'

(However I have found that in fact they were found close together, if it's the same children, and it's highly likely they were the same. Additionally, some of their clothing had been taken from the scene, but most likely by an altogether different predator; a man by the name of Robert Jepson, a convicted child killer who, three decades later confessed that he had killed them, more of which later.)

The witness continues, 'May 11th, 1974 (two years later) myself and fellow BUFORA Investigator were driving by the area when we stopped and got out. We gazed over in the direction of the copse. We talked about that time. Looking around casually, I noticed what looked like a person standing by the trees on the ridge and called my friend's attention to it.'

'The ridge and tree line from our position is approx 400yds. We decided to have a closer look and reached into the car for our respective binoculars and then focussed on the figure, standing completely still, facing us. Through the 10x50 binoculars the figure was indeed perplexing. It was approximately average human height, and wore what could only be described as a black gown which reached from the neck down to the ground. It had long blonde/white hair but what disturbed me was that it had no facial features at all. My fellow investigator was just as agitated as I was at seeing this. Talking between ourselves as to what the hell was going on, he said, "Look to the left of the trees." I raised my binoculars and followed his pointing finger.'

'There stood an identical being. Swinging back towards the right, the first 'being' had gone, then left again, but that 'being' had gone too. Totally bewildered I lit a cigarette and leaned back on the car. My friend shouted "Look, along the hedgerows." These were about 200Yds away from us. Now this sounds funny, but was only funny looking back afterwards; at the time I was seriously concerned. Along the hedgerows ran, at a pretty fast pace, a white roughly human shaped 'thing.' It had no features at all. This was joined by another nearby. These were simply aimlessly dashing about.'

'My friend said "****" and got back in the car hurriedly, saying, "Lets get out of here."

We drove away and stopped in a car-park a mile or so away and discussed what we had just seen. It was dark by now and we decided to drive back. We got out of the car and with our binoculars, stood at a fence, looking towards the area and scanning the copse. After a short time I noticed a small red light just above the trees, it was a slightly bigger red light through the lenses.'

'Early next day, Sunday 12th, my friend and I visited the then BUFORA NIC Ken Phillips, gave him our reports and detailed what we experienced. We talked of other witnesses, mentioning the two young girls and the man standing outside his house. Onto possible photographic evidence; even though the camera my friend used was an Instamatic 126 cartridge camera, not best type for night shots, there was a slim chance something might show up in print. We discussed possible inside sources for development of the film rather than risk a commercial company. I suggested Omar Fowler, a prominent Ufologist at that time in Surrey. The Film cartridge was sent to him by Ken with a covering letter explaining the event. We waited anxiously for results.'

'Tracing the two girls was impossible, we drew a blank with the man too, when we knocked on his front door and explained who we were and what we wanted he stood expressionless and said he was sitting watching TV all evening, said he never left the room. When I told him I saw him outside his house watching the 'display' he emphatically denied it and told us to **** off and never come back!!'

'This was not looking good, we returned to Kens place and stated we drew a blank with other witnesses. He suggested any other possible evidence, traces maybe at the site. It was agreed we would return to the area and have a good look around. In the bright sunlit afternoon walking up towards the ridge we stopped at the copse and could not resist a quick peek inside, the place where 4 years earlier those two small bodies were recovered. At the ridge, by the trees I looked around and smiled, looking up at the end trees and I smiled more. Branches lay on the ground, branches were damaged on the trees too. I took many color photographs of this damage. Fully detailed reports were drawn up by myself and separately by my fellow investigator, and presented to BUFORA along with pictures. I also sent a similar detailed report with pictures to the Ministry of Defence and to CUFOS in the USA. (This report was later detailed in the CUFOS backed report by Ted Bloecher, 1976 "Physical Trace Cases".

'A week or two after sending the film to Omar we received bad news. Evidently the film had jammed in the cartridge, we had no photo evidence!!'

Interestingly, in an old Journal called 'The Voice,' from 1997, the same man explains being at a base for his job as a security officer, being tagged with a chip, and of being aware of programmed generated life-forms, as well as the development of A.I. capable of reading every person's thoughts and emotions. Possible? Recently, suggestions were made about the true reason behind Jade Helm being an A.I. program, by whistleblower 'DJ' on various podcasts including John B Wells 'Caravan to Midnight' episode 309. Interestingly, this UFO experiencer's claims were made many years before this.

While his account of the faceless entities and strange red light in the woods is perplexing and disturbing, the big problem with the account of the two missing and returned children is that 30 years later, a man in prison confessed to their murders. Already imprisoned for the murder of another child, Ronald Jebson confessed after three decades that he had done it.

Whille no names are given in the UFO experiencer's reports of the two children found dead, they were found in the same proximity as the bodies of 11 year old Susan Blatchford and her friend 12 year old Gary Hanlon, who were discovered in the copse in March

1970. The likelihood of it being a different pair of children is extremely small. The case became known as 'The Babes in the Woods,' and had remained unsolved for three decades until Jebson, already serving a life sentence for the 1974 murder of eight-year-old Rosemary Papper, confessed to the murders.

Certainly, the UFO researcher didn't know, when he wrote his account of the alleged mysterious goings-on in the copse that summer, that a human killer would later confess to the crime. So, was he mistaken in his first-hand account of a UFO sighting at the reservoir and the subsequent find of the two children with burn marks? Had he 'guessed' at the reason for the discovery of the dead children and presumed that they had been the victim of alien abduction? He stated at the time that the names of the children were not released and that the parents were forced to move away from the area and not talk to anyone about what had happened. Did he have inside sources? Or had he naievely manipulated the facts to suit his own agenda? Of course, it's perfectly possible that he did really see UFO activity at the reservoir and woods, and the strange creatures, and as a result of his UFO sighting, he believed that the two children had died of alien intervention.

According to the accounts of Newspapers at the time when the two bodies were found, the names of the two children were clearly stated, and the coroner's official report stated that the children were lying next to each other but the cause of death could not be given other than "unascertainable," due to the degree of decomposition that had taken place. They were found partially clothed, and the coroner speculated that some of the clothing had been 'removed by foxes.' To some of the police however, the coroner's statement defied the clear evidence that the children were victims of homicide, because of the circumstantial evidence found at the scene. For one, the girl's underclothes were missing. The unofficial view of most authorities however, was that the children had simply gotten lost and died of exposure. Neither Nipper Read, the legendary policeman who put away the infamous Kray Twins, nor the parents of the victims, believed this and were reported as firmly believing it was murder.

Of course, the one thing on the UFO investigator's side is that the police tracker dogs and cadaver dogs had been over that site repeatedly and found no scent. The children lived a quarter of a mile from the site. On the other hand, the killer could have placed them there at a later stage; although the bodies had badly decomposed and from the coroner's report it seems that the belief is they were at the site for some time.

There's also the very slight possibility that the UFO researcher is referring to two other children, as their names were redacted in the letter he sent to the Ministry of Defence. One other possible clue to back up the UFO investigator's belief of a non-human agenda perhaps inadvertently comes from the policeman Nipper Read, who would later say, "Many senior officials at Scotland Yard tried to dissuade me and were insistent that it was a just tragic accident that the children had become lost and died of exposure."

Like the UFO researcher, he also simply couldn't believe that two children could die of exposure in the summer months and within a quarter of a mile from their own homes, and so close to a street with houses on it nearby.

Why were 'many senior officials' so keen to press their opinion on the policeman trying to solve the case, trying to get him to drop the investigation and convince him that two children could die of exposure during a warm summer?

UFO researchers and conspiracy researchers would perhaps suggest that this could indicate that there really was some kind of cover-up from those in high places, because they did not want the public to learn of the visitation from malevolent alien entities.

Perhaps it could also be suggested, that as in the case of the other two murdered girls in the woods near to the Air Force base, this killer too was a convenient patsy?

Interestingly, it appears that there could be another altogether different reason why the police didn't want the case investigated and the killer caught. In another twist, in 2014, Don Hale of the Daily Star Newspaper wrote a story about the killer's prison cell-mate, which could reveal another possible explanation for what was quite possibly a cover-up, again, if at all credible. His cell-mate made the extraordinary claim that he had been deliberately placed near to the killer Jebson, in prison, for the specific purpose of trying to extract information from him about his involvement in a paedophile ring. The cell-mate went on to claim that the child killer had told him he had been a chauffeur employed to drive children to sick 'auctions' in mansions in the Surrey countryside, where high level people placed 'bids' for the children.

"Killer worked as chauffeur ferrying innocent youngsters to be abused at sick orgies by high-ranking officials, it was claimed." The article came out amid the on-going allegations and investigations into the child abuse scandal in the UK, involving 'the establishment,' but that has so far also failed to find any firm proof of it existing, although conspiracists will say that too has been covered up.

The likelihood is that both the murderer and his cell-mate were lying about this too; however if he was lying about this claim of being a chauffeur to child sex trafficking for 'the establishment,' then it serves useful if only to show that the murderer could potentially also have been lying about killing the two children.

Again, was it human or alien abduction and murder? That is for the reader to decide. These cases seem to lead from one twist and turn to the next, and almost always appear to go even further down the rabbit hole as they say, when looked into more deeply. Do they begin as naive beliefs and germinate into the wildest of speculations founded on nothing more than imagination and supposition? Or are there kernels of truth within?

Why is it, that when these stories are looked into, very often they lead to a very strange set of circumstances that appear to be revealed as the story goes deeper and deeper?

There's someone else who talks about the alleged abduction and murder of humans in woods and forests too. This time it's another 'whistleblower' called Corey Goode, who in his own words, describes himself as having been "identified as an intuitive empath with precognitive abilities," who subsequently "found himself recruited through a MILAB program at 6 years old." He says that he was trained within this program for a decade. Towards the end of his time he claims he was assigned to a "rotating Earth Delegate Seat in a "human-type" ET Super Federation Council."

Talking with David Wilcock, on Jimmy Church's Fade to Black radio show, (September 13, 2015, on YouTube) he made some astonishing and very disturbing comments and allegations of his own regarding the possibility of sinister things happening to people in woodland and forested areas.

He talked of "body drops" in "areas used by different ET groups." He said, "they drop the human bodies back from high altitude down onto the ground."

"A lot of them are in National Parks and other isolated areas. A lot of Park Rangers know about this. A lot of these are federal employees that are deferred to these areas. There are areas where different ET groups come in and abduct human beings. They do experiments that go wrong, or utilize different parts of human beings for different things, and the humans perish. They drop the bodies in dumping areas, like a serial killer would do, and these are areas that seem to be used by different groups but they're common areas spread out across the planet and a lot of the time these bodies are dropped form high altitude. The Federal agencies go in there and investigate it, keep it quiet, clean up the situation and then they do not inform the families that they found bodies, and they do not return the bodies back to the families."

Is there any possibility that this could be true? Different rogue groups of alien races snatching up humans, and then discarding them in the woods and forests once they are done with them? Certainly Corey Goode thinks so.

Referring back to the previous incident discussed, about the two children found dead in the woods by the reservoir, and what UFO researcher 'Barry' also claimed was of his subsequent encounters with 'MIB's,' as a result of his investigations; when he said,

"They're menacing only if you show them fear; if you stand up to them and don't appear disturbed by their appearance, it's like a process kicks in as though they're not programmed for that response and they 'shut down.' If fear and stress is shown when under their attention, their pre-set programming of intimidation will continue."

There's another highly controversial figure, a man called Dan Burisch, who some believe and many others don't, when he makes the claim "MIB's are J-Rods that 'wear the dead' and act as 'guards' of 'timelines,' to ensure that sensitive issues are not disclosed that could change our future history to any considerable degree. Their bodies belong to human cadavers."

Are there really 'Rogue Aliens' called J-Rods who transfer their 'intelligence' or 'consciousness' into dead human bodies to facilitate their mobility here on earth? His claims are terrifying, but of course, what it lacks is easy-to-verify evidence, as is so often the case. Dan Burisch claims to have encountered J-Rods at Area 51 and said this was what the Men in Black were. Could it be at all possible in any way? An alien race, abducting both children and adults, killing them, and wearing their skin as masks to hide inside?

One man claims a similar thing, only this time it concerns the Black Eyed Kids, or B.E.K's. On a variation of Burisch's theme, John Kettler of johnkettler .com, claims that B.E.K's also seek to get inside you; only this time, they are after your soul.

This man claims to have some inside info on the 'Black Eyed Kids.' According to him, he's a man who has a background of 'a lifelong study of military technology and black programs, covert operations and espionage.' He says his father was an engineer who worked on 'Top Secret' projects for the Air Force and CIA. He says that he himself then worked for Raytheon for a decade as a military analyst working with 'Spooks.'

He claims, on johnkettler.com, that from his insider sources, he knows who these mysterious, menacing and sinister black eyed kids are.

"The power of the dark is way beyond our simple understanding. Information recently received indicates a very real and potentially mortal threat to anyone who encounters them. Is this serious? - They eat souls and destroy that which makes us who we are. They are not human. Their appearance is merely a disguise to make them approachable. They are slaves of the Reptoids and the Cabal, and their task is to 'clean the planet up.' -It means, ridding the planet of us." Crucially, he describes humans as their "prospective dinners."

"What follows," he says, "is from 'sensitive sources;' because people are essentially absolutely dumbed-down about the realities within this sector of creation, we cannot ascertain what their possibilities might be. Because they need to be invited in, they are giving 'lip service' to the laws of the creational, where one must agree to be consumed. To the predator, being invited in means you agree to whatever comes next."

He continues, "An inquiry to the ET side" (implying this is from an ET source) "indicates that these (BEK's) are of an insect nature. They are here to get rid of humans. Although you can't see their true form, they are not human."

His 'source' continues, allegedly having come into contact with them.

"They wanted me to know who they were. They spoke in their childlike voices. I said, "I know you're not children." Then came a more masculine voice. They said they were soul eaters."

Then the source said he asked them to show him their true form.

"It was one of the most stupid things in my life. I will never forget it. It was a triangular form with the top point being the head. I could see sucking tubes. I don't dare to guess their true size."

The source came up with further details indicating that these sentient beings are apparently winged.

Kettler himself recounts an incident that he is aware of where the occupants of a rural house let in some of these black eyed entities. The result, he claims, was not good.

'They (the people) were 'incubused;' their souls were taken and a holographic imprint of their soul was merged with an incubus. It's hard to tell the difference between the clone and the original. These entities then, have a good cover. One of my contacts knows people who have been incubused. She could see a subtle but definite change in them."

In other words, he claims that the people were infested by entites that took over their souls and merged their personalities with their own. Those who knew them could tell they were 'changed' somehow, though they didn't know it was as a result of a visitation from the BEK's, but they knew the people were no longer the same.

"They were inhabited and possessed by the non-human entities who had knocked on their door. My contact could tell the difference in them by their lack of interest in certain matters; and a lack of responsiveness to matters that used to be important to them."

How utterly chilling. Or is this man's information again just another crazy sci-fi story? Many people have claimed to have had encounters with these entities but not given in to letting them in. There seem to be no accounts from those who have let them in. Is this because it's too late; they have been changed now and do not know it?

In June 2014, Cliff at Pararational blog received a highly detailed account of what happened to a 26 year old man called David, who works at a college in Michigan.

David writes, 'I'm an average man. I don't believe in the paranormal. I love to camp and hike and I was at Sleeping Bear Dunes just out of season in late August. At the Ranger station, I used the bathroom. Coming out of the stall, there are two kids standing there. I wash my hands and glance in the mirror, and see they are looking at me. My spine tingled with fear. They have completely black eyes. No whites in their eyes at all. I froze in fear. They looked around aged twelve. Fight or flight took over.

"Can you help us?" said one of the boys. Despite my fear, I wanted to help them. I stood thinking I wanted to; until finally my head said, "No," and I left.

I remember thinking that I was certain I was going to die as I turned my back to go; that they were going to rip me to shreds. I'm six foot! Anyway, I get the hell out of there; I can't bring myself to look back.

I drive to the camp-site parking lot, and then it's a forty minute walk to my camping spot. When I get there it's completely empty of campers. After building a fire, eventually I sleep.

As dawn came the next morning, I felt foolish for the fear I'd felt yesterday. A calm guy, I couldn't explain the intense dread I'd felt when I'd seen the kids.'

He spends the day hiking and driving into town for dinner. On his return, he heads out on the 40 minute walk back to the camp. A storm has come and it's dark now.

'As I walked, my dread grew. I walked and stopped every few metres to look round with my headlamp, but saw nothing; then I walked on and just knew someone was there, watching. Then, I turned around, and there they were, both motionless. I can't put my terror in words. The boy came toward me. My light flashed across his face; his grotesque eyes.

"Help us."

I couldn't breathe. The boy moved closer. The other boy was slowly circling me.

"We're lost. Take us with you."

My flight response hit as the boy reached for my hand. I recoiled. I ran. I don't look back. I don't know if they're behind me or not; all I know is that I must run faster.'

Back at the tent, he eventually manages to fall asleep.

'I thought it was a nightmare at first, when I heard the unmistakable voice.

"Help us."

I couldn't help it. I screamed.

"Please let us in."

"No," I screamed, again and again and again. Then I waited for death....'

Though he stayed awake all night, they didn't enter his tent; instead they stood menacingly outside of it.

'It's been almost two months since this happened, but I still remember it all like it was yesterday. I haven't gone camping since, and I don't know if I'll ever feel safe hiking again..."

Did this really happen? Only the man in question knows but the account is certainly a chilling one.

Chapter 2:
Magickal Working, Art, and Ancient Races

There is another man who also claims he has the answer to the origins of the B.E.K.'s. It's a fascinating version of a possibility and in my researching of it, it led to a story with a compelling mix of the occult, the esoteric, Art, and ancient races.

In November 2015, one of Amadeo Modigliani's paintings *Nu Couche*, or, *Reclining Nude*, distinctive for its beautiful shaping and those endless dark eyes, became the second most expensive painting ever sold, at a price of $170 million.

His *Bust of a Young Woman*, too, had those deep black eyes. His painting of Anna Zborowska was the same; the blackest of eyes. When he painted Jacques and his wife Berthe Lipchitz, again they were painted with jet black eyes; no sclera at all.

Why would he paint jet black eyes with no white in them? Why were their entire eyes black?

Italian painter Amadeo Modigliani, (1884-1920) would say, "When I know your soul I will paint your eyes," but one researcher makes an astonishing and outlandish claim that there is quite simply much more to this than that statement of intent.

The famous painter's Mother, Eugene Garsin, began keeping a diary in 1886, when the artist was just a small boy.

"We know very little about his life and work from 1886-7, and the problem of sources now becomes particularly acute." This quote comes from Jeanne Modigliani, from her own biography of her father, the famous Italian artist, and his life was indeed shrouded in elements of great mystery and intrigue, but in his mother's diary, according to one researcher, there are allegedly some very interesting clues that he believes may possibly reveal what really influenced the artist to paint those black eyes.

In the diary she writes, "Isaac (his grandfather) is getting too attached to Dedo (Amadeo), taking him everywhere. He is taking him to the temple but not our temple."

This is according to researcher Danti Sartori, who has kindly given me permission to include his extensive research into the diary in this book. Sartori explains that in the late 1990's, he spent several years tracking down the diary and exploring it, searching for something specific; something which would, in his mind, lead to a startling revelation on the origins of the phenomenon of Black Eyed Kids.

Quite possibly the temple that Amadeo's mother refers to is a Masonic lodge, as researcher Mr Sartori points out that Amadeo's grandfather was allegedly a Mason and his own father, Solomon Garson some say was possibly a 33rd degree Mason, and furthermore, Sartori alleges he was involved with the Illuminati. Of course, this is impossible to verify; however, it is true that in the Italian town where they lived, in Livorno, 18 of the Masonic lodges, that's half of the total number of the 34 lodges in Italy, were based in the town, so it was certainly an important centre of Masonic activity in Italy. Whether he really was involved in the illuminati however, is another matter and one that cannot be proven by Sartori unless evidence is furnished, despite his own confidence. This too applies to the Diary. What Sartori goes on to claim quite possibly may be entirely fallacious, but it certainly makes for compelling reading.

Sartori spent a significant amount of time in the Library Biblioteque d'Alcazar in Marseilles, in the South of France, where the diary of Euegene Garsin was said to be located. He had been translating it and reading it, interspersed with frequent and often long trips away during the second gulf war, as a member of the Italian Special Forces. When he managed to return to Marseille the last time, he discovered that the diary was gone from the Library.

He explains all in his videos on YouTube, AHK: app 59 – Black Rain.

"During the 1980's I spent a lot of time researching the life of Modigliani. Unfortunately where I was living at the time the resources were somewhat trivial. I knew there were several private collectors who had Modigliani's private writings. I contacted them asking if I could have a look at them but was refused. I also knew that there were 2 libraries in Paris and Livorno where he was born that had some of his writings. I contacted them again, again was refused.

But my life has a way of taking me to the right places at generally the right time and so in the mid '90's because of work I found my self living in Marseille. And why is this important? Well Marseille happens to be where Eugene Garsin was born and raised- his mother. I tried to find out about her, then one night I went to a bar where I used to hang out under my apartments, which turned out to be owned and run by the local mob. Anyway, I got talking to an Irish guy (I'd been going to the bar now for six months) and chatting and I told him what I'd been trying to do or find and he said "Oh I heard something about that a while ago," "I said, ' Really?' He made a phone call and a local mob guy arrived and tells him his boss had some papers either related to Modigliani or his family in his possession and said he would talk to him about what I was looking for."

A few days later this Irish friend from the bar tells me the boss did not have the papers anymore; that he had given then to one of the local Libraries Biblioteque de Alacazar. (mafia philanthropy!)"

That was how he managed to get his hands on them, Sartori says, and that was where he spent most of his time. After having to go away once more for his army work however, when he returned again he found them gone from the Library. It turned out that the mafia boss had requested them back, but according to Sartori, he allowed him to go to his house where he kept them, to continue with his research.

It was what he says he found in the diaries that led him to make the most astonishing claims.

Inside the diary, he alleges, are the following entries,

'July 1889. "Amedee (his Uncle) and Isaac; I know they want Dedo (Modigliani) to be one of them. I know they want him to be the new face of the movement."

Sartori comments, "the illiuminati have always sought to recruit and promote those at the fore-front of art and music. They have always chosen/recruited artists; because it influences a whole generation."

His inference, from having studied the alleged diary, is that the men were actively looking to groom and place Modigliani at the prominence, to promote their hidden agenda to the masses.

If Sartori's findings are correct from the diary, it would seem that Modigliani's mother was against this and concerned enough by it that she planned to take him away. (Other historians will say that it was because the child was sickly and she took him away to recuperate.)

'August 1889. "Now I know that I must take Dedo out of here. Isaac is furious about it. He wants him close by more than ever."

'September 1889. "I must take Dedo out of Lisvorio – I must, I must. I don't want him to become them- no; not one of those soulless eyes. I've seen them, they are close. Closer. My son is going to paint them."

Who is Modigliani's mother talking about him painting? Who is *them*? Her father and brother? Or someone else? Paint who? Why does she describe them as having '*soulless eyes*?'

She does take her son away, first to Tuscany and then on to Florence.

In 1901, researcher Santori remarks that there was a UFO phenomenon occurring in Northern Italy, in Tuscany, called locally 'The Lights of Berberiro.'

In the diary, according to Sartori, the young painter's mother refers to them in a disturbing way,

"The lights of Berberiro seem to follow us everywhere we go." (In Tuscany)

Then, "We are in Florence now. So are the lights. What could they be? Plenty of people ask the same. Dedo seems amused by them."

If this is really true, why and how does this tie in with her son?

It gets worse; they seem to be a constant presence now;

'1901. "We are in Rome. Dedo is increasingly interested in the lights. Last night I found him walking around in the garden. I swear I heard him laughing. "

'1901. "We are in Venice. I know what I'm seeing and I have seen them. I am not going mad. They are here. I am sure Dedo speaks to them at night."

'1901, "I sat outside Dedo's room all night. Just before sunrise I heard a voice, saying "paint us, paint us."

Amadeo was just a small boy at this time.

Who are they? Sartori says that around this time there were "many strange phenomenon" and "many 'alien abductions' taking place, mostly aimed at young boys and girls."

Toward the end of 1901, according to Sartori, the diary allegedly continues, in a fatalistic and ominous tone,

"I must return home. I know they are part of his life now. Maybe even more than myself. Those deep black eyes, dark like the night...and they are young, so young; Dedo's age, even younger."

Clearly then, from the diary that Santori claims to have uncovered, according to his supposed findings, not only was the boy's mother trying to get her young son away from the alleged Masonic-Illuminati influences of her Father and grandfather, in order to stop them from inducting him and using him as a public face of the organisation, but it seemed she and her son were being 'followed' by unidentified beings; children with 'deep black eyes, dark like the night;' beings that wanted him to paint them.

Given that many of his subsequent paintings were of those very distinctive and sometimes disquieting black-eyed people, the inference here is very obvious; that the entities who visited the boy when he was young, led to his life-long pursuit of depicting these black-eyed entities, these 'soul-eaters;' the black-eyed-kids in his portraitures.

Is there any way at all that Sartori's claims about the diary are really true? Besides it being a fantastical story, is there any grain of truth in it? Mysteriously, between the 1901-1903 period of his life we have 'the missing years,' where allegedly nothing is written in the diary. What happened to him during those two years?

As one art critic, Michael O'Sullivan in the Washington Post has written, "What is perhaps most unusual about his portraits is not the elongation of their features, but their eyes. His portraits are like masks, both in their reductive sameness and in the emptiness of their eyes. His gift lay not in the painting of eyes, but of souls."

But whose souls was he painting? Through Sartori's decades of research into the diary, he clearly feels that it was the souls of the black-eyed creatures who had stalked him, accompanied by the strange lights in the sky and the stories of missing children happening in the area at the same time. He also clearly feels that there is some link between these Black Eyed Beings and the Masonic-Illuminate desires of the artist's patriarchs.

The resarcher makes for a compelling case that the reason for Modigliani's black eyed portraitures is because he was made to paint them; he was made to depict the entities that appeared to him night after night as a boy, and Sartori believes they are tied in with the accounts of people going missing and the lights. On the other hand, we do not have the diary to verify this, and they could also just as easily have been manifestations of the occult and of demonic origin. Or, they could simply be the product of Sartori's wild imagination.

Looking more closely at Modigliani's childhood however, it was unorthodox to say the least. With his grandfather, Isaac, having both possibly a deep Masonic and Illuminati connection, the boy also came from a line of Jewish scholars with an in-depth knowledge of the ancient texts and the magickal practices within them. Then there was his aunt who was said to have been entrenched in 'mystical practice,' and another account from Modigliani's daughter, who cites the time the boy painted two skulls on a bookcase in the house when he was 12 years old. In his own words the boy described how the woman's skull was a symbol of "love in all its destructive power," and the man's, a patriarch with long divided beard was "the male succubus, which is what he too often is." The male succubus presumably being a demon. This is quite deep for a 12 year old, and perhaps a good reflection of the spiritual nature of his upbringing.

His own letters in later life perhaps also could be construed as containing hints,

"Dear friend,

I write to pour myself out to you and to affirm myself. I am the prey of great powers that surge forth and then disintegrate."

He could of course be referring simply to his artistic nature; or he could be referring to something more supernatural.

Like many artists, during his lifetime he was never wealthy and famous, though he was well-known in Paris. It was after his death that his paintings began to sell for astronomical sums of money.

He knew mostly poverty when growing up, although his father was a money lender/banker, and according to Jeanne, his daughter, his mother would say during the times the bailiffs came to take away their possessions, that 'the Modigliani's used to be bankers to the Pope.'

Jeanne corrects this often uttered phrase by saying that in her opinion, it was more truthful that the family once loaned money to a cardinal associated with the Pope, but whatever the finer details, the family believed themselves far richer than their circumstances proved them to be.

Although, perhaps they were not so wrong about their position within the banking world. A distant cousin of Modigliani, Leah Modigliani in the late 1990's developed the term 'Modigliani-Modigliani measure', also known as 'M-squared;' which is a measure for 'risk adjusted performance' which seeks to adjust leverage artificially then measures the returns. She developed it while she was in charge of 11450 brokers at New

York's Morgan Stanley. Clearly she was very well placed within the banking industry, although that could have had nothing to do with family connections.

The family were Sephardic Jews, and Jeanne says that the practice of passionate Talmudic learning and discussion was very much alive in the household she grew up in, with her paternal aunt, after Modigliani died and her own mother committed suicide the following day.

It was from Modigliani's great-grandfather on his Mother's side that the Rabbinic Judaism came from, as he had been a commentator on The Sacred Books and had founded a school for Talmudic studies. The Talmud normally alludes to the collection of writings that make up the Babylonian Talmud. Within these texts are sources of high Magick, although at the time written, the practise of Witchcraft was forbidden. Especially in the Babylonian Talmud, a great number of the passages allude to magick, which, according to the 1906 Jewish Encyclopedia, by Joseph Jacobs and Ludwig Blau, "furnishes incontrovertible evidence" of Magick's wide-scale use.

Although forbidden to be practised, because it was so widely used, it was deemed necessary for those in positions of authority, such as members of the Judiciary, to have a knowledge of this Magick.

In fact, 'this ingrained belief in Magick infected even the scholars, who would sometimes counteract the black magic with white.' Furthermore, it says, 'They were even able to create food when they needed it. Some scholars were adepts in the black arts, and the Law did not deny its power. Many scholars consumed men with a glance, or reduced them to a heap of bones.'

The great-grandfather of Modigliani then, had an in-depth knowledge of magickal practices, as did perhaps his own son, Modigliani's grandfather, Isaac, with some biographers of Modigliani alluding to his grandfather's ready use of Magick and Spells. He was also described by many as a very cultured man who could command many different languages.

Isaac came to live with Modigliani when he was just a child, after Isaac suffered from what Jeanne describe as a mental breakdown following the failure of his banking business. It's hard to verify whether this is really so from other sources, but what is apparent is that Isaac and Modigliani became inseparable. Modigliani's own father was seldom there, usually away in Sardinia where his businesses were located.

The other version is that Isaac, Modigliani's grandfather, had gone to live with them after the death of first his wife, then their daughter, Clementine, who had lived with him. This is where perhaps things get interesting, though there is more than one path to take when it comes to attempting to get to the bottom of the biggest enigma surrounding Modigliani. It wasn't so much him; rather, it was the subject of his paintings. They were all of people. Invariably they all had long cone-shaped heads, and very often, the blackest eyes imaginable. Some had white sclera; but many others did not. Why was that? Why would he paint jet black eyes with no white at all? Why were their entire eyes black?

Almost all art commentators fall back on Modigliani's own statement, "When I know your soul I will paint your eyes."

His daughter, who was a babe-in-arms when her father died, mentions Clemintine, Modigliani's aunt and "her marvellous black eyes," as Jeanne describes them, and says that she was a woman who was "entrenched in a mystical religion."

Did she inspire Modigliani perhaps?

On the other hand, Jeanne also speculates that a close friend of the family, Leone Opler's daughter, who she says had a pale elongated face, could have been the muse for the great painter. "The girl cannot remember him ever painting her," however.

Modigliani's main patron when he became an artist was French Physician, Paul Alexandre. He wrote to his sister after the artist's death. "In his drawings there is purification of form. He reconstructed the human face in his own way by fitting them into primitive patterns," and there are no sinister implications in his mind as to where the inspiration came from, believing them to be 'from African masks.' However, he does add, "Max Jacobs," described by many as 'the poet-alchemist' of the time, was someone who "stimulated Modigliani's taste for magick and the occult, which came out in the cabalistic signs that appear in a few of his drawings. Like Jacobs, Modigliani took a keen interest in the mystical connections between material and spiritual realms and mystical correspondences."

One of his drawings, 'Tete de profil,' belonged Paul Alexandre, and bore inscriptions next to it written by Modigliani.

The inscriptions are a poem, translated as; 'Just as the snake slithers out of its skin So you will deliver yourself from sin. Equilibrium by means of opposite extremes. Man considered from three aspects. Frustration!'

Is this the three Talmudic aspects? Or the Body, Soul, Spirit connection? Or the 3 stages of Freemasonry?

Alexandre's son, Noel, an ecclesiastical historian, says "We know very little about the place the occult sciences held in Modigliani's life. This drawing is rare for it captures unusual inscriptions on the right side of the sheet" and to him, it clearly "offers proof of his (Modigliani's) personal commitment to the esoteric."

He continues, "Paul Alexandre, who was never interested in the esoteric, was nevertheless struck by these mystical correspondences that his artist friend was searching for in alchemy. These brief lines are particularly precious to us, even if, in the absence of any other documentation, we are unable to understand their full meaning."

Of course, 'esoteric' does not necessarily mean anything sinister by its definition, but it does mean 'understandable only by an enlightened inner circle.'

Mystery seemed to enshroud Modigliani's life, and he appeared strongly attracted by the occult. 'I am the plaything of powerful forces that are born and die in me,' Modigliani once wrote.

Meryle Secrest, who wrote a biography of the artist, says, "Modigliani came from a family interested in the occult, and Beatrice Hastings (a lover of his) was into Theosophy, among other things. As for alchemy, he once worked alchemical symbols into a statement he appended to a drawing, so he was certainly familiar with the subject."

When selling the pencil sketch by Modigliani, of Conrad D Moricand, a previously unpublished artwork from one of his sketchbooks, the Lempertz Auction

House wrote that the artist had been close to Moricand, "an astrologist and occultist," and had painted him several times.

Art historian and expert on Modigliani, Marc Restellini points out the 'motifs' he found in the artist's works that feature the occultist Conrad Moricand. 'An oil painting depicts Moricand, as do at least eight other drawings, and inscriptions and comments by Modigliani bear witness that the artist was obviously not averse to the occult and was interested in esotericism.'

In art, a 'motif' is an element of pattern in an image, or a symbol that is commonly used so that it becomes iconic.

Writer Leslie Camhi comments, about a series of sculpted busts he created, that they 'viscerally evoke its origins in occult practices that fascinated the artist, who is rumored to have embraced their strange geometries by candlelight.'

Not only then are there multiple sources who overtly make claim that there is evidence of the artist's fascination with the esoteric, occult, and magick, but there appears to be another researcher too who makes the claim, whether true or not, that "Modigliani, as with Dante Alighieri, was also Illuminati. Dante Allighieri was an initiate who wrote *The Divine Comedy* to perpetuate Illuminati secret codes," says Alex Ribiero.

He continues, "The 1925 book The Dante Esoteric, written by Rene Guenon, shows that these Illuminati codes are placed, since antiquity, into monuments, architecture, movies, music, literature and art. That's what Dante did with the Divine Comedy, starting with its structure; a poem in three parts, of Hell, Purgatory and Paradise, under the three Illuminati pillars, The Unholy, The Initiation and Enlightenment, with messages in the form of codes included in the stanzas of the poem. Modigliani, was initiated in the occult at 5 years of age by his grandfather Isaac Garsin as well as made literate in this by his grandfather, and his mother Eugenia Garsin, with The Divine Comedy."

"All the symbols found in the pictorial part of 'Velieri to Livorno' are skulls, snakes, horses, demons, fly, boat; all these symbols in the are Illuminati codes."

"Velieri to Livorno' is a painting that Robiero has been in the process of trying to have authenticated; a painting that he attributes to Modigliani, and presented to the 3nd Latin-American Symposium on Physical and Chemical Methods in Archaeology, Art and Cultural Heritage Conservation, in 2011. It is still awaiting attribution and may well turn out not to be by Modigliani.

"Like all Illuminati, particularly Dante Allighieri, Modigliani recorded Illuminati codes subliminally or disguised, without calling direct attention to them; hidden information. Like Leonardo Da Vinci," who he says, "was also Illuminati. Modigliani also wrote Letters and Numbers underneath the paintings."

So there is speculation and indeed possible clues that Modigliani was influenced by the occult and perhaps indeed even had ties to the illuminati. These observations of course however do not indicate a necessary proof of Sartori's research and the notes he claims are in the mother's diary, nor do they indicate that Sartori is correct in his alleged 'proof' that Modigliani was directly influenced supernaturally by BEK's, who he clearly believes are of extraterrestrial origin; but it does make for a compelling possibility if nothing else.

Interestingly, sculptor Jacques Lipchitz, who wrote of Modigliani after his death noted that his mistress, (who later threw herself off a balcony after his death) "was a strange girl, with a long oval face which seemed almost white rather than flesh color."

Was Modigliani simply influenced to paint the black eyes of his figures by those around him? It's clearly quite possible; but he had started painting the black eyes long before he met his mistress. Is there anything in Dante Sartori's theory that Modigliani was visited and influenced by visitations from BEK's and those strange lights in the sky? Without the diary it is very hard to say, but something influenced him to paint those unique black 'soulless eyes.'

As Sartori alleges, his mother writes,

"I know what I'm seeing and I have seen them. I am not going mad. They are here. I am sure Dedo speaks to them at night. I sat outside Dedo's room all night. Just before sunrise I heard a woman's voice, saying "paint us, paint us. I know they are part of his life now. Those deep black eyes, dark like the night...and they are young, so young, Dedo's age, even younger."

While perhaps the research of Sartori should be dismissed as mere fantasy and just a fascinating but impossible story, there is another interesting link that he highlighted with regards to possible missing children and child abductions at the time, and the influence of the occult and supernatural. As researcher Alex Robiero as well as Sartori also pointed out, the artist became a connoisseur and admirer of Dante Allighieri. At 13 years old, Modigliani could already recite the Divine Comedy from memory, which is no mean feat.

This is corroborated by a close friend of the artist, sculptor Jacques Lipchitz, who wrote,

"Now, I always associate him with poetry. Is it because it was the poet Max Jacob who introduced me to him? Or is it because when Max introduced us in Paris in 1913, Modigliani suddenly began to recite by heart the Divine Comedy at the top of his voice? More often than not he would recite by heart their verses."

Around the same time, there was another boy who could also do exactly what Modigliani could do. It wasn't just Modigliani who seemed to have the remarkable and exceptional talent for reciting by heart the verses of Dante's poems. There was another little boy who lived with his brother in the village of Ruvo di Puglia. At the same time that Modigliani was allegedly, according to one researcher, receiving visits from Black Eyed Children, two young boys, Alfred 7, and Paulo, 8, began to disappear in seemingly impossible ways. The affair involving the boys was a long one and it was documented and recorded by the no less than the physician to the then Pope Leo XIII, as well as later by Charles Fort, Lombroso Cesare, Lapponi Giuseppe, the Occult Review and and the 1906 Annals of Psychical Science.

It seemed that it began after the parents of the two boys unwisely allowed them to take part in a séance that they attended. A few days after this, Alfred began to have inexplicable bouts of extreme tiredness, during which it was said that he frightened his parents by speaking to them in languages they had never heard before, and in a voice which did not seem to belong to him. He spoke as though he was reciting verse, and it sounded as though he was speaking Latin, or Greek. Soon, he was reciting cantos from Dante's Divine Comedy, in Latin. He had never studied Dante's Divine Comedy, and he had never been taught Latin.

The family was so concerned about the changes in their son that having sought religious counsel, they sent him to a boarding school where he remained for the next two years. It hadn't just been the strange voice coming out of him at home; there had been numerous 'miracle' manifestations of food and other items which had appeared from out of no-where.

At the school, he disconcerted everyone. Any time anyone went to ask him a question, he would answer it even before the question came out of their mouths; and on a range of complex topics of which the boy was too young to have studied.

When he accompanied three of his school professors to another séance, they sat around the table with a triangle formed of paper to be used as a planchette for the Ouija board. They began the session and asked if anyone was there and they received the reply, 'Yes; but you must use a triangle made of wood.'

One of the participants replied that they had no wood, to which the small boy told the group that there was a wood triangle in the kitchen, that he said he had got from the carpenter's shop. They looked in the kitchen and found a perfectly constructed wooden triangle. The boy, as far as they knew, had never been to the house they were in, nor the carpenter's shop located in another village.

The little boy was returned to live with his family. What happened next was an increase in unexplained phenomena. There were strange and frightening noises inside the house, glasses were thrown by invisible hands, the furniture was shifted around without anyone touching it. While this all sounds ridiculous and a story based in folklore perhaps, it was in fact documented by among others, the chief Doctor to Pope Leo XIII. The ongoing saga was also documented in the national newspapers.

The local priest was called to help and he conducted an exorcism but in his presence, the furniture continued to be thrown around and glasses smashed against the walls. The table with the holy water was thrown across the room.

The priest left in helplessness and the phenomena continued unabated. The little boy continued to speak in a voice that did not belong to him, and in languages the family did not know. Then the voice told them that it had been sent from God to drive out the dark forces in the little boy. After this, sweets and chocolate began to be found around the house, yet the family had not purchased any of the candy. One night the little boy, after falling into a trance, told his parents "a terrible battle is taking place between Good and Evil."

The oddities didn't stop there; in fact, they got even more bizarre. One day the little boy was with his brother when they were found at a Convent in another town. It was 9.30 am. They had been at home at 9 a.m. The town was more than 30 miles away. It was an impossibility for them to have got there. There was no car to have taken them. A few days later, the family were having lunch around 12.30pm when the father realised they had no wine. He asked the older brother to fetch some and bring it to the table. After thirty minutes the boy had not returned and the father asked Alfred to go and look for him and bring him back. At 1 p.m. the two boys were found in a boat on the sea outside of the port of a neighboring village. The fisherman had suddenly found them on his boat and was shocked, and the little boys had started to cry. Confused and dumbfounded by their appearance, he took the boat back into the harbour and a coach and horses took them back to their home. They did not return until 3.30pm in the afternoon, the ride back being a considerable journey.

Their parents could not understand how they could both possibly have got on the boat, nor how they could have reached the port in the 30 minutes when it was further away than that. It seemed they were being instantaneously transported.

Franz Hartmann, a medical doctor but also a keen scholar of the occult, was one of the many who took an interest in their strange experiences. The boys had been thoroughly medically examined by doctors and scientist and no one could come up with anything that would explain how they seemed to be getting teleported. Hartmann wrote of the case, "They were taken away in some mysterious manner and found fifteen minutes after, in a place 55 miles away."

According to Aaron, researcher of esoterx. com, the doctors and the scientists tried to test for various medical explanations, such as "ambulatory automatism" or "muscular hyperesthesia" neither of which really offered anywhere near a reasonable explanation, and the newspapers who were covering the strange incidents interviewed eye witnesses of the events and felt it was "inspiegabile;" that is 'unexplainable.'

The theory most easily accepted by the scientists and religious experts of the day who looked into the matter, was that it had to be a case of 'ambulatory automatism;' that is, a form of nervous disease where the subject suffering from it is overtaken with an irresistible urge to run!

The Annals of Psychical Science wrote in 1906, that even allowing for the possibility that the two boys might have run flat out for a long distance, they felt the argument did not hold water when applied to the fact that the boys appeared to have run nearly ten miles in just under thirty minutes. They add also that the boys were seen by no witnesses along the route at all. Besides which, one time Bishop Bernandi Pasquale had locked the two boys in their room, sealing the door and windows, yet within a few minutes the boys had somehow disappeared from the room.

A well known criminologist Cesare Lombroso also studied the case, interviewing those who had seen either the boys before they went missing or where they turned up, and he too could find no distortion of events, nor any logical or reasonable explanation. The boys' experiences stopped suddenly when they hit puberty and never occurred again.

Calling to mind Modigliani's paintings with the black eyes and strange elgonated necks, English essayist in the 1800's, Maurice Henry Hewlett, wrote Lore of Posperine, which features a true account of the strangest of 'creatures' with an elongated neck, and the sinister results of it's appearance.

"The facts were as follows. A Mr Stephen Mortimer Beckwith, 28, clerk in the Wiltshire & Dorset Bank at Salisbury was living in Wishford. He was married with one child.

At approximately 10 pm on the 30th November, 1887, he was going home after spending the evening at a friend's house. It was a mild night, with rain and a wind was blowing. There was a quarter moon and it was not completely dark. Accompanied by his dog, he was riding a bicycle. He stated that he had no difficulty seeing the road nor the stones on it nor the sheep in the hillside. He recalled quite clearly seeing an owl flying.

A mile or so along and his terrier dog ran through the hedge and ran barking up the hill. The man imagined he was after a hare and called him, but the dog took no notice and ran to a gorse bush then stopped, paw uplifted and watching it intensely.

The man watched him for some minutes, dismounting from his bicycle. He could see nothing up there himself but the dog was in a state of excitement. It was whimpering and trembling, and his master decided to take a look at what was causing this behaviour in his dog. The dog would not take his eyes off whatever was up there.

Now standing just behind the dog, the man looked but could see nothing there. He had no stick and imagining it could be a drunk man in there in need of help or a rabbit caught in a trap, he urged his dog inward, but the dog wouldn't move and eventually it began to howl.

It shook his owner, who because of the isolated location and a 'mysterious shroud of darkness,' wanted nothing more than to leave the spot, but he now couldn't get his dog to leave. Finally, he braved it and put his two hands inside the bush to try to feel for what was in there. It was during this fumbling that he suddenly saw a bright pair of eyes staring back at him, and a pale face.

He found his voice and asked who they were, what was wrong, why they were in there, but no answer came back. He tried to reassure them that he meant no harm to them.

There was no movement at all of the features of the face. It was a very small face, "about as big as a large wax doll's. It was longish and oval and very pale. I could see its neck and it was no thicker than my wrist. I would have said it was a girl had it not been for the size of her and her face. It was, in fact, neither fish, flesh, nor fowl. Strap my dog had known that from the beginning, and now I was of Strap's opinion myself."

In his mind he called her 'a foreigner;' for he had no other word for it. To him she was something he could not define. Her face was that of an older girl, a late teenager at least but her size was under three foot. She couldn't seem to understand what he said to her and said nothing back to him. Her clothing was odd too. It seemed almost like it was made of cobwebs.

It was all of this that made him suspect her of being 'something outside experience,' but this was just the beginning. Suddenly he heard footsteps and a torch coming up the hill toward him and it was the local policeman. The man told the policeman immediately that there seemed to be some kind of foul play at hand, because he had found this tiny girl and didn't know what else to say. The policeman followed the direction the man's head went in, as the man indicated the girl he now had in his arms, having pulled her out of the gorse, but the policeman couldn't appear to see anything in his arms. In fact, he made a joke and walked back down the hill.

Now the man really did know something was wrong. However, he didn't feel he could just leave her there in the rain and darkness and so he took her back home with him.

When he got home his wife was waiting anxiously at the front door looking out into the dark, worried that he was so late. When he began to explain what had happened, it became evident that just like the policeman, his wife also could not see the girl. In fact, she placed her hand on the handlebars of the bicycle where he had propped up the girl to ride home with her. His wife's arm went straight through the girl.

"It was as if my wife had drilled a hole clean through the middle of her back. Her hand went through the skin and bone and dress; how I do not know."

He could not bring himself to take this invisible creature into the house with them, so he put her in the dog's kennel.

"I blame myself for it, myself only," he was later to say.

He kept the small 'child' in the kennel for almost six months. She shared the kennel with his other dog. He fed her though she never ate any of it. She spent her time dancing and playing with the two dogs; then later she would play with his own child, a four year old girl. The little girl would never tell him that she was playing with the other strange girl, but it was evident they were playing together, though the four year old denied it. She too could see the strange girl, though his wife never did.

"We might have been spared if, on the night I brought her home, I had told my wife the whole truth. And yet, how could I? Is not that an absurdity? Yes, but the sequel was no absurdity."

In the Otautau Standard and Wallace County Chronicle, Volume V, Issue 231, 5 October 1909, his tale continues.

'Now I come to the tragic part of my story and wish I could leave it out, but beyond the full confession I have made to the police and the newspapers, I am to blame. On the 13th of May, she and my daughter disappeared."

The search party covered a radius of miles, searching every fold of the hills, every hedgerow. He told his wife, the Reverend, and the police about the strange girl he had been harbouring. He told the newspapers.

"In spite of my wife's absolute incredulity, and scorn, I repeated the tale to the Chief Inspector and details soon got into the local newspaper and the London journals."

Neither the Newspapers nor the police at the time accused him of any involvement in his daughter's disappearance; They believed his testimony.

"I don't doubt now that she was bewitching my daughter. She had been crowning her with a wreath of flowers she had made for her."

His daughter was never seen again.

Chapter 3:
Caves, Caverns, and Screams

The Green Children of Wolfpit is a mystery that sounds like a fairytale and yet several texts from those times report it as being genuine.

It occurred during the reign of King Stephen in the 12th Century, outside of the village of Wolfpit, in the rural county of Suffolk, England. Farm workers were toiling in the fields during harvest one day when two small children were spotted emerging from a deep ravine that had been dug for the purpose of trapping wolves on the edge of the forest that lined the fields.

As the workers watched them getting closer, they were shocked and perplexed by their strange appearance, because their skin appeared to be green. Not only was their skin a glowing green hue but their clothes also did not appear to be the same as everyone else's.

They appeared strange and unfamiliar in both fashion and material. The children too looked just as perplexed and confused as the farm workers did. They looked all around them as though they didn't know where they were.

Not knowing what to do, some of the farm workers led them into the village. They had tried to talk to the two children, who both looked to be under the age of ten, although they did not look like normal children, because of their skin colour. When the farm workers had tried to ask them if they were ok, the children did not seem to understand what they were saying to them.

The children answered them, but they seemed to be speaking in a language the farm workers could not understand. It wasn't a different dialect or accent; it was an entirely strange language that they had never heard before.

In the village, the villagers too could not communicate with them and eventually they took the two children to the home of the Lord of the Manor. His servants brought food and water for them but the children refused to eat any of it.

This went on for several days, with the villagers growing concerned that they would end up starving to death and it was only when they took them some freshly harvested green beans that the children accepted them and ate them hungrily.

Sadly the two children seemed to be very depressed and unhappy in their new environment, and after a few months the boy died. The girl adjusted more easily to her new life to a certain extent, in that she managed to learn the language everyone around her spoke and was then able to at least communicate with people. Of course, everyone wanted to know where they had come from and now she could tell them.

She said that her and her brother had come from the land called 'Saint Martin,' where everyone lived in permanent twilight and everyone was as green as them. She couldn't say exactly where that land was but believed it was across a river. She said that they had been looking after their father's cows when some of the cows had gone into a cavern and the children had followed after them.

Inside the cavern she said that they heard the beautiful sound of bells ringing softly and the sound encouraged them to seek its source. They walked deeper into the dark cavern and arrived at an entrance that glowed so brightly it stunned them and they lay down.

She says they lay in a daze for a long time until they found themselves in the field with the farm workers. They had been trying to escape the cave and return home but had found themselves in a new land instead.

Two original texts from the 12th Century seem to verify the strange story. One is by a Monk, William of Newburgh, who wrote,

'It was as if they had been fashioned from summer leaves and soft meadow grass; their skin was green as was the strange hue of their eyes."

He goes on to note that their land, according to the little girl, saw no sunlight, and when they came to the bright sunlight at the exit of the cave, it overwhelmed and stunned them. They were struck terrified by it; they did not know what it was.

"I was overwhelmed by the weight of so many and such competent witnesses," he writes.

In the 1977 November issue of FATE magazine, another strange tale was told.

"Recent violent occurrences in Veracruz again have brought the Chanques into prominence.

Apparently, the story in question features a little boy who was abducted and held in a cave in a thick forest.

Senora Cirila Laguens, a shop owner, told the magazine,

"My 3 year old son Ramiro, he wandered from home. He was missing for six days. He was found by the Chaneques. Instead of telling us, because they are very timid, they told our neighbour's young son, that he could be found in a cave ten miles away."

"A search party went to the cave and found my son asleep inside. Although he'd been gone for several days, he was in perfect health and not hungry or thirsty or unhappy. He quickly told us that he had got lost near a river and five little men had found him. They had taken him and given him food and milk and then he had slept. When he woke he said he found himself in a cave. He said the little ones stayed with him and played with him."

Knowing that no-one will believe her son's story, the mother continues, "Of course, my son, not wishing to be told off for not staying near to home must have invented the tale, not wishing to be chastised; but it's not that simple. He is a little young to invent this. Moreover, the entire hillside where the cave is, right up to the mouth of the cave, is covered with extremely dense shrub that's five feet tall with spines and limbs. My son's rescuers had to cut their way into the cave to reach him. They all suffered bruises and scratches; some even had puncture wounds on their arms and legs. My son, who was barefoot and bare-legged, was found without a single mark on him. It's also foolish to say that his friend had brought the food and drink to him for those days he was missing, not just because of the inaccessibility of the cave, but because it was an 18 mile round trip."

The editor adds, 'this is similar to the accounts of caverns east of Phoenix and south-western New Mexico where they have been seen by ranchers standing like sentinels on the ridges and have reportedly led children out of dangerous areas and fed them.'

Says FATE magazine, "This next account was given us by Senor R. Gutierrez. He told us that in the summer of 1970 he was walking with his little nephew Arto in the Forest, near Mixtequilla in Veracruz. Though his nephew was walking right by his side, he suddenly became aware that the boy was no longer there. As soon as he realised this, he immediately began to search the area around him, but could find no sign of him and no answers to his calls.'

'Making a return to the nearest village, after a lengthy search on his own, he gathered together a large search party and together they returned to the spot and carried out an extensive search, but they had no success in finding the little boy. As a result, the man was arrested for murder, but while he was awaiting the start of the trial, his nephew reappeared. It had been more than 30 days since he had vanished, but he appeared completely unharmed and looking as though he had been well looked after, fed, and kept clean. He simply walked back into his house to the shock of his parents. The boy was completely content and not in any distress at all.'

'Said his uncle, "When we asked him where he had been all this time he told us, 'I've been with the little men. They gave me honey and milk, and we played lots of games."

The murder charge was dropped and the authorities took no further investigation into whether he had been abducted or not.

Says FATE, "We checked out the story with the police and they confirmed to us that this was indeed the story."

A less happy tale is told by a one Ludovig Granchi who too had gone into the woods outside of the city of Rio de Janeiro. He'd gone into the woods because he was curious about a sudden sighting of strange lights in the woods. It was late at night and as he walked into the woods he began to hear what sounded like a hoard of crickets all around him. Without any warning he suddenly found himself in the middle of a group of 'men' of small stature who appeared to be wearing some kind of uniform. "They all had green eyes and blonde hair, white skin, and were very thin. They had wands with light coming from them."

He said they seized hold of him and took him into a cave in the woods where they forced him to lie on a slab of stone. The noise coming from them, like crickets he said, was "incessant," as they used their wands on him and 'inspected and examined' him. Sometime later he managed to find his voice and ask them if they knew who he was, and one of them replied in a high pitched voice that they did, and told him his name.

Eventually, after a thorough examination, they allowed him out of the cave, and he said that though he was safe, he felt 'strange and confused' for at least a week.

Those who follow Richard Sauder's work know he has chronicled alleged secret underground bases across the U.S. Along with the reporting of what he said are huge and sinister bases, he also chronicled the strange story of a man called George Haycock who, in the '60's, told him that he had found a shaft in a boulder field outside of Burley, Idaho. 'Native American legends tell of a demonic race who emerge from the caves and capture their families. George reported coming under strong psychic attack and being given the impressions of terrible 'evil activities' taking place under the ground. The shaft he discovered led to an ancient tunnel through a crawlspace with tunnels that branched off and a cave in which he attempted to dig. While in there he reported experiencing 'unusual resistance' when trying to dig. Later he would tell friends that 'someone' was trying to blast the tunnel to seal it up. The police classified him as "a druggist." He reported receiving a death threat by letter, which told him to 'cease and desist.' He was shortly after this found strangled in his home.'

In 'Project Red Book,' author Branton, who as outlandish as it sounds, claims to be a "sleeper agent" who was programmed with fractured personalities to serve the 'Bavarian-Gray collective,' alleges that in France, a woman Doctor told him she was abducted and taken into caverns where she found herself amid other human prisoners, who were being raped and tortured by 'cannibal beast-men.' She was held there for months, she claimed, until 'pale-skinned beings' in 'metallic' uniforms freed them all. She said that she learned the pale-skinned beings were sent to this planet to observe "the coming war between surface armies and the beasts of the caves, who have ancient technology which they use against humanity for their own pleasure."

The account was collected by him from 'The Hollow Earth,' by Warren Smith and was originally recorded by a German occultist who documented various similar accounts and put them into "The Messerschmidt Manuscript."

Also collected by Branton, according to the now defunct Search Magazine, in 1964, a woman called Ervin Scott wrote to them to tell of how she had heard a telepathic message, that it seems came to her as though she had somehow accidently picked up on it, and rather bizarrely, it appeared to be an urgent warning 'about a woman who was abducted into caverns beneath a Church in Boston 3 weeks earlier.'

Even more bizarrely, she then claims she heard another voice, which 'breaks into the transmission and says, "Don't believe her. Don't you know this is a trick and a lie?" and then warns her, "Keep quiet about this."

In an area of boulders, caverns and tunnels, the Black Mountain region in New South Wales, Australia, is said to be a site of supernatural phenomenon, with numerous accounts of mysterious disappearances of both people and animals.

There have been reports of people disappearing never to be seen again. Police and trackers who have set out to search for them have sometimes themselves also disappeared, giving Black Mountain the name 'Mountain of Death.'

It has a strange geography, comprising of enormous boulders that are black and formed from magma millions of years ago, and the indigenous population refuse to go near it. Just its appearance is sinister.

There have been a range of different types of reports, varying from strange sounds coming from beneath the ground, to sightings of human-like shadows. Even pilots flying over the area have reported disturbing air turbulence which has made flying difficult until out of the area. Alien researchers say it is a place with 'UFO activity.'

Underneath the boulders are numerous tunnels and caverns from which are said to come sounds of moans and crying. It could be the flow of air moving naturally through the place, but the indigenous people believe it is home to an ancient underground races. There are numerous tales of people seeing fleeting ghostly black shapes moving across the boulders.

One of the stories relates to a man named Harty Owens, who was out on the mountain looking for his cattle after they had mysteriously disappeared. He didn't return back to the farm so his farm manager Hawkins went to the mountain to look for him, taking with him some of the local police.

A pair of policemen went down into one of the caves to see if he had somehow fallen inside, but only one of them came back out. He was shaking and ghastly white and he was never able to talk about what it was he had seen down in the cave. Neither the other policeman who had gone down into the cave, nor the farm worker was ever found.

A Corpse in a cave? On April 15th, 1988, a High School senior left his Linwood home in Kansas, driving his mother's car en-route to a friend's party in a rural wooded area nearby. It's thought he disappeared around 2am, although no-one could confirm seeing him leave. On the night in question, Randy had left his parents' in the early evening and driven to a friend's house, then on to a garage where his soon-to-be graduation present, a car from his parents, was being restored.

He arrived at the bonfire party at a farm in the rural spot about 5 km from his own home, at around 10pm, where up to 150 other people were gathered. The mother of the boy whose party it was said that Randy 'had trouble walking but didn't appear drunk,' and also that she, and others, never saw him with a drink in his hand. He'd bought some soda at a gas store before arriving there. However, by the time he went to leave, one of his friend claimed he was too drunk to walk. His friend told him not to drive and amid the crowd they got separated after that. When his friend tried to find him again the car was gone and so was he. Neither the car nor the boy have ever been seen again.

His parents called the police by 2 am, worried as he had never before been late for a curfew. The police went to the site of the bonfire the next morning, but it had already been cleaned up and they couldn't find any evidence to suggest what might have happened to the boy. Then the farmhouse burnt down not long after.

Then a couple of months later, a man went to the police with a rather strange and disturbing story. He told them that he had been kidnapped by a satanic cult and held captive in a cave for fourteen days, and even worse, that he had seen a corpse hanging in the cave while he had been there. He thought it might be the missing young man. The man said his kidnappers had threatened to cut off his left arm and had then pointed to a dead man's body hanging in the gloomy cave. The Police went to the location the man described to them and searched the cave but they found no evidence of any crime taking place there.

The conclusion the police decided to make was that the man had hallucinated the experience while under the influence of drugs. The police hadn't gone immediately to search the cave however; they had gone some time at a later stage. The cave has since been bulldozed, with some locals claiming it was at the demands of the police that it be done.

A close friend of the missing boy also went to the police to tell them what he had found. He took them to the banks of the Kansas River where a severed foot lay. The foot was not the missing boys however, and then this friend then died a few years later.

In 2002, the case was reclassified as a homicide and three men were arrested for his abduction. However, they were soon released without charge with the police saying they had made a mistake.

The case has many strange and unusual elements to it, with some claiming that his friend's death was suspicious, and then there are the internal police reports that kept turning up in the mailbox of his parents. The boy's father said he didn't know who they were coming from but felt it could be from a member of the investigation team who was trying to tell him something or show that the case was being botched.

In 1993, a man purporting to be a research journalist offered his assistance to the boy's parents and spent several months without pay interviewing those who had been there that night and others who might have known something about the case. The man went by the name of Terry. According to The Mirror, the local news journal for Tonganoxie, Kansas, in its article entitled List of Oddities, 'an independent investigator called Terry Martin was subsequently found shot to death along with his wife. Topeka police ruled it a "murder-suicide." Others are not so sure.... and there are still no answers about what happened that night, the alleged mysterious cave, and the fate of the young man.

Within the Bridgewater Triangle in Massachusetts is Freetown Forest. Bridgewater triangle is an area said to be rife with reports that range from alien activity to unidentified cryptids that lurk at night and frighten the unsuspecting traveller.

The Freetown forest is even darker, as it's believed a lot of the activities that occur inside of it are of a more human origin, but heavily linked to satanic worship.

The site of quite a few murders, there has been rumors of satanic cults using the forest as their conjuring and hunting grounds.

A teenage girl called Mary Arruda was found tied to a tree in the late 1970's. She had been left for dead after having been snatched and taken into the forest. Another time, a man was found terribly beaten inside the forest, and told investigators that he had been attacked by a group of Satanists who had tried to kill him. Another man was once found naked with an array of stab wounds. He had fled the forest and run to the nearest house for help.

Those who go into the forest, perhaps unaware of its black magic reputation are said to have experienced some terrifying things; of hearing demonic, disembodied voices near to them and yet there is no-one in the forest with them that they can see.

One man fishing in the nearby pool claimed that one day in early evening he saw a group of people walking toward him. He turned back to watch his fishing rod and when he turned back to look at the group of people they had gone but he saw them out of the corner of his eye, in a completely different location and one that would have been impossible to walk to in the amount of time he had turned his head.

Car drivers passing by the forest have also reported strange events, of not only seeing dark shapes in the forest but of those same shapes running alongside their car and keeping pace with them.

Back in 1972, in Springfield, New Jersey, Jeanette DePalma disappeared.

She had once had a drug and alcohol problem, but now she was clean and it was said that she dedicated her time to helping others struggling with the addictions, and had turned to the Church. She disappeared suddenly without any warning or indication that there was anything wrong in her life to make her leave town without telling anyone.

No sign of her was seen for nearly two months until a man was walking his dog in the local woods and his dog ran back to him with what looked like a large bone. On closer inspection it turned out to be a decomposed human hand and part of an arm.

The horrified man immediately called the police and the authorities set about searching the rest of the area for the remaining body parts with a team of bloodhounds.

It did not take long to find the rest of the body and it was a woman, laying face down and fully clothed in the woods.

Because she had decomposed so badly the forensic examiner was not able to determine how she had died, but obviously they believed it was a case of murder. She was positively identified as the missing girl, who had only just become a teenager that year.

There was no actual evidence left at the scene of the crime, except for what was at first dismissed; until the police looked at the ground more closely and realised that the logs and branches that surrounded her body, which looked like they were just natural forest debris that had fallen or gathered there quite naturally, were in fact not there by chance. According to the writers of Weird New Jersey, they looked as though they had been placed there in some kind of strange pattern almost suggestive of some kind of occult or black magic satanic ritual. Later, some of the police reflected that they were arranged around her almost like a trapezium that surrounded her, encasing her in a 'box' as though a coffin, with a cross formed at the top of her.

Was this some kind of altar or coffin formation that had been ritually created they wondered? Perhaps what also made them think in this way were the rumours in the area that it had been a site for witches and black magic and covens for many years.

Gossip started to circulate in the town of dead animals being found in mysterious ways in the same woods, and of cult activities happening there at night.

When reporters came to the town many local people spoke to them but did not want to be identified and gave vague accounts of possible covens and scarifies taking place. They seemed almost too frightened to go in to detail.

Was this just local rumour and superstition? Some even said they knew that human sacrifices took place in the area. Some even said they had accidently witnessed such things happening. The police received many anonymous letters and telephone calls but they never gave any names of suspects.

People began to speculate, was her new found religious belief and church attendance the motive? Had someone taken against her because she now went to Church? Had they felt affronted and provoked and as a gang, abducted her in revenge and to inflict their own warped beliefs on her?

Then there was the local library where the librarians had been forced to keep the occult books in a locked cabinet because so many of them on the subject had been stolen from the building.

With no suspects and no-where to turn, the crime eventually went cold and after that of course, new rumours started that the authorities knew who was involved and they were deliberately or quite possibly being forced to cover things up; being given orders from those higher up than them or by those they were in fear of.

The more level headed citizens agreed it was quite possibly a cover-up, but done so to preserve the good name of the area and not to alarm the people any more than they already were.

What is for certain, from the reactions of those living there at the time, they were definitely frightened of something.

Chapter 4:
Silence & Blood-curdling Screams in the woods

Mysterious stone formations and circular trenches are embedded in the ground in Ballyboley Forest, in Larne, Northern Ireland, giving rise to beliefs that it's an ancient Druid site and a gateway to "the Otherworld," according to the Celtic tradition.

Although forest workers of the Park Service maintain the landscaped trails for visitors to use, there are other natural paths that never seem to need maintenance, that stay oddly clear of any foliage or branches, their paths always mysteriously remaining clear. It's said that the local people do not like to venture into the forest.

People who do enter it often return describing the eerie feeling that they were being watched. There are many tales of people seeing shadow figures standing amongst the trees, wearing dark robes, and their heads covered by cowls. There are ancient books which describe the mysterious disappearances of people who never returned after going in the forest.

In 1994, newspapers reported the strange incident of a couple who were walking through the forest when they suddenly heard screaming. Moments later a 'large dark shadow' appeared in front of them making them run off in terror.

In 1997 two men reportedly said they were walking through the forest when they heard a flapping sound that was very loud. They didn't know what it was so tried to ignore it and carried on walking.

Moments later they started hearing what sounded like a woman crying and moaning in pain or distress. Concerned for her state of health, they quickly tried to find her but could see no-one nearby.

What they did see however were trees smeared with blood all around them.

Running in fear, as they fled they both glanced behind them and to their horror both believed they could see a group of figures in dark cloaks standing where the trees were.

Found on Reddit ten years ago, one girl described how she had camped out in the forest for part of the Duke of Edinburgh Award scheme.

"On our last night there, we were camped in a clearing where there were no trees. As the light was fading someone in the group said they could see people moving around in the trees. We went toward the trees to check it out, thinking it was another group who'd got lost, but there was no-one there. We didn't think any more of it and went back and were having hot chocolate around the fire when someone else noticed there was some movement in the trees again. This time, the figures seemed to be holding torches, but this is where it got strange. Instead of modern flashlights the figures seemed to be holding branches on fire. There were four figures.

Later that night one of the group who lived on a farm and would therefore know a bit about this said that, after the figures had vanished, they could hear sounds like an abattoir; of cries and squeals.'

Posted to an outdoors forum in 2009, is another chilling and inexplicable experience.

"We were fishing on the shoreline of the river one night. We had a fire going, and we were talking and had some beers when all of a sudden we all stopped talking suddenly.

We all felt as if something or someone was staring at us from across the river. We tried to shake it off with macho humor when the most bloodcurdling sound erupted from over there, that froze us all.

The sound was unlike anything any of us had ever heard. It made every hair on my body stand up. The only way I can describe it is it sounded like a person being gutted alive. No words, just this high pitched bloodcurdling scream. Nobody moved or said a word. Just as suddenly a second scream came with even more force than the first.

We sprinted to our firearms in the truck, then sat there in silence, our eyes fixed on the other side. We never did figure out or even guess what was there on the opposite bank.

The village of Pluckley and the woods surrounding it is the most haunted area in England, according to the Guinness book of records.

Frequent blood curdling screams coming from the woods are heard by the villagers but whenever they have gone into the woods to find out where the screams are coming from they never find anyone there.

People who have gone into the woods have said they were followed by an ominous black shadow and the sound of footsteps have suddenly been heard from behind them, but when they turn around no-one is there.

In one spot in the woods back in the 18th Century, a highwayman was once caught. He had attempted to hold-up a coach of passengers but it seems that some of the passengers fought back, and they used his own sword to impale him to a tree then tied him up and left him there to die of his wound. It's said that he now roams the woods in search of vengeance.

In one of the lanes in the woods, sometimes the apparition of a man's body hanging from the tree is seen and it's said to be that of an old school master who committed suicide there; or was taken there and killed. The true version is not known as one day he simply went missing and was never seen again until a few weeks later when his body was spotted hanging there in the woods.

At a disused clay pit in the woods, an industrial accident resulted in a worker being trapped by a fall of clay, covering him over and leaving him there to suffocate to death. Ever since then, walkers have spoken of hearing a man's screams and pleas for help.

In recent times, one female visitor was with a group of friends there when they had a strange experience.

'The atmosphere was a happy one and we heard all the birds and animals in the woods; but as we got deeper into the woods, it seemed that all the animals had gone quiet. In fact, it got so quiet you could have heard a pin drop. The girls in the group, including me, got spooked by this and we decided we wanted to go back to the car. We turned round and went out of the forest, but the boys carried on, going deeper into it.

About 15 minutes later they came back. They were running. They jostled with each other trying to get back in the car as quickly as they could and their faces were ash-pale. They started the car up and turned it to leave but it stalled suddenly and then we all saw this huge black mist coming from the woods, coming in our direction towards us. It looked like it was 'walking' toward us.'

S. Vince sent in her story to the *Haunted Writer* blog.

"In the summer of 2010, I was in the woods behind our parent's house with my brother in Butler County, Pennsylvania. I was 20, my brother was 18. We're both confident people, and I believe in logic. I don't get spooked easily because I think there's an explanation for everything; or at least I did.

We took an axe; we planned on having a bonfire and were on the quest for firewood. It was a warm sunny summer day and the wind was low.

We'd been in the woods about a thousand times. We started to venture deeper into the woods; something we'd done every time we had been there. We both said how loud the sounds were; the insects and birds and other animals scurrying around.

After about ten minutes, we found a few trees that looked dead and ideal for firewood and we went off the path into the thick.

As soon as we stepped off it things around us changed. I noticed straight away that all the sounds had changed. The birds had gone, and the insects and clouds came out of no-where.

Slightly unnerved, we kept working; but that did not last long. After maybe 30 seconds I started to get a sensation I had never felt before.

Every hair on my body began to stand up. I looked at my brother and could tell something similar was happening with him.

We looked around us but everything appeared to be normal; no other people, no animal. Our eyes met again and we sort of laughed it off, but we were not quite sure what was going on.

After what seemed like an hour, but was probably seconds of looking around again, we got back to work. No more than ten seconds later, the most frightening thing started. The wind stopped. All sound was gone. It was the kind of quiet where you hear your heart beat. The air was dead. I had pins and needles along my spine. I don't know what it was; all I know is that it was behind us. We could feel its presence and it did not want us there.

I exchanged a frantic look with my brother and we both get out of there and got back on the path. As we turned to look back around, a feeling of pure dread struck me. I felt like I was about to vomit. I felt like I was paralyzed in a vacuum, seeing everything around me frame by frame. I looked towards my brother and he snapped out of whatever trance we had been caught in, and we began sprinting towards home.

To this day, I don't know what happened. All I know is the next time I opened my eyes, I was running behind my brother on the way back to the house. I had no control over my body; it was just running, getting me out of there. To this day, I don't know what was out there.

Anonyn writes,

'I was not far from an area called Blood Mtn. I've camped and hunted in this area for 25 years. Never had anything like it before. I was hiking along a trail in the forest with two firearms. Suddenly I got really scared. All the hairs on the back of my neck stood up.

The ridge line of the hill was up about 700 yards ahead and something was up there tracking me. I turned back immediately, but even when I was back in the truck, I was still scared. I still felt something very close to me. I've never felt anything like it.'

Jim writes in forum dcexposed,

'While hunting in Georgia. In a familiar area, suddenly there were no normal sounds and no wind. Something came rushing toward me, pushing the plants aside.

I turned away before it reached me, had my gun aimed ready. Did this save me? There was a very bad feeling of danger. I pushed through a brier to get out of there. Something told me don't go back, just keep moving forward. To this day I feel I came close to something evil. My Brother and Dad had been calling me and sounding the car horn just 200 yards away. I never heard them.'

Among the foothills and pines of East Kentucky, on November 21st 2003, a University psychology professor and his two sons were driving home when they saw a bright light in the Western sky. There was a soundless aerial object, hovering over a nearby field. They stopped the car, and according to their testimonies, given to investigators Kenny Young and Donnie Blessing, something unexplained was in the sky. At the top of a hill ridge, not far away, they could see the white hovering object.

Getting back in their car with a growing sense of apprehension, unsure of whether the object had spotted them, they drove back to their nearby home and when they reached it, they all went to the second floor to look out of the window. The object in the sky hadn't gone anywhere.

At the same time, a woman in a nearby home was outside hanging up Christmas lights on the exterior of her house when she saw an object in the sky bobbing up and down. She became frightened and told her young daughter to go in the house. As she too turned to get back inside the house, the object began to lower and the lights coming from it turned to orange and red and as it touched down on the ground, dogs nearby began to howl. Suddenly the object shot off like a dart and disappeared into the sky. Immediately after it departed, blood-curdling screams could be heard from the fields or woods nearby. It was a woman's voice screaming, "Oh God, please somebody help me, Oh God, No!"

A man living in a house that was next to the field, called 911 immediately. He told the dispatcher he could hear a woman screaming and sounding like she was struggling. He told the dispatcher he'd gone outside into the field with his spotlight but couldn't see anyone in the field or the woods.

He later told the investigator Donnie, "It sounded like somebody being hurt; it sounded like somebody being ripped apart."

A police search yielded no answers. They searched the field and the woods. The witness described the area of his residence as isolated and surrounded by fields and woodland.

In UFO researcher Kenny Young's subsequent investigation of the incident, he did an internet search the following evening to find the telephone numbers of anyone who resided along the lane which was closest to the field and woods. He found one household and called them on the phone to ask them if they had heard or seen anything. The man who answered it was called Professor Virgil Davis and he was a British-born college lecturer at Kentucky Community College in Ashland.

The man told him, "I was here when the screams were heard; there were loud, blood-curdling screams but no-one could find anything."

The researchers asked him if he had seen anything, to which he replied that he was driving at the time with his two teenage sons. He said the object moved "like a humming bird," and was oval with white light and the size of a pea at arms length. As it was dark, approximately 9.30pm that winter, it could be seen very brightly against the night sky, and was quite high until it started to move, "coming down, and moving in increments."

He told the researcher that they stopped the car and got out to try to work out what it was, and they were sure it was neither an airplane nor the aurora borealis. "There was no explanation for this, and I didn't know what we were looking at. I had some concern that it could have spotted us, or that it might."

He told the researcher of their short drive back to their house and their observation of the object from their second floor window, during which time they watched it descend and settle in the field nearby as its color changed to red and it appeared larger. "Everything was real quiet, then everything went crazy."

He described how his dog tried to break its chain outside the house as it went into a frenzy, as did other dogs in the area.

He said they became "dumfounded" when it suddenly shot off with great acceleration.

"I was very reluctant to call the police, and I wasn't going to report it," the witness continues, "but right after that my sons went outside and heard screaming. It was a woman's voice. They got in the car and called me within minutes saying the screaming was coming from the field where it had come down."

At that point, the witness called the police. "20 minutes later there were about twenty police officers and a rescue squad in the field. Others had heard the screaming too."

One of his sons repeated what he had heard coming from the field by the woods. He said it was "a desperate scream, blood-curdling. It was a female voice that kept saying; "Help me, Oh God, Help me!"

The witness told the researcher that he was not the one who made the report to NUFORC and that someone else must have. The NUFOCR report corroborated the sighting, the screams, and the search squad combing the field and woodlands. That report states: "report of a female crying for help x3. From two witness. The fire department was asked to begin searching with the thermal imaging camera. No results found.'

Says Young, "The report of desperate, blood curdling screams coming from a woman crying out, "Help me, Oh God, Help me," give this case a disturbing sense of dread. Clearly there was something taking place and this report raises the spectre of reported UFO/human abduction."

Chapter 5:
Non-humans in the woods

A report received by MUFON of an incident in February 25, 2011, was sent in by a witness who was in the Ansonia Nature centre, 150 acres of wooded hills, in Ansonia, CT.

"As I sometimes do, I was walking in the Ansonia Nature area late at night. This time, as I was on the way back through the woods, all of a sudden a deer ran frantically across in front of me, as if it had been spooked by something, and it skid and fell. I don't think it was me that spooked it. It felt like a weird quiet; like something is about to happen.

I walked on, taking a path on some open terrain next to the woods. While I was walking, I wasn't focusing on anything in particular, then suddenly my eyes focussed on some entity approximately 25 metres ahead, crouched slightly in a very aggressive stance and staring right at me.

When I first saw it, it was like I already knew subjectively that it was ET of some kind. Yes, there are many other logical explanations possible, of course, but I will elaborate on the strangeness anyway, even if it wasn't extraterrestrial.

The figure was glowing a blue-gray. It was as though it was naked. The head was over-sized, the arms and legs were skinny. It seemed human-like in form; athletic, ready, aggressive and focussed. I didn't see any eyes yet I could tell it was staring right at me and we were like two animals in the wild in a stand off, guarding our terrain.

It felt as though I'd stumbled into this entity too soon, like it was waiting for me but I'd noticed it too soon and was too alert, and it turned very athletically and ran at full speed into the woods. I heard the bushes as it took off into the woods.

I told a friend who said it was just a person. This is very possible but there was a strange energy involved in the encounter and I had the sense I might be ambushed by it. There was an extreme sense of danger and tension. I walk in the woods at night regularly and deer approach me or stalk, and all other kinds of sounds and I don't feel scared. If it had been a person, it would had to have had an eerie aura about it to scare me. And what on earth would cause him to stare at me overtly aggressively then run full speed into the woods. Crazy right? I went back the next day and looked at the exact spot. All the way along the path is very thick shrubs, trees, bushes; it's all tangled and I thought, how did it run full speed through this? It seemed impossible. It would have been impossible for me to go through it.

The strongest impression I get is that I felt it had been watching me, waiting for me, and I wasn't supposed to see it so soon. When it ran off, and this is very important, it was not in a scared manner but in a very confident and regimented way, and in a way that let you know it meant business and wasn't scared, but more that, it needed to get out of the area for some reason. Afterward, I was glad I went back the way I did, sure that if I had not I could have been ambushed. The feelings and impression I have is that this entity was something other than human.'

In Albert Rosales seminal work ufoinfo.com/humanoid, which lists sightings of entities of unknown origin worldwide since as far back as the 1870's to the present day, one of the accounts he has collected comes from John Colombo's book 'UFOs over Canada.'

It happened in a place called Onion Lake, in Wapiti Lake Forest, British Columbia, Canada, back in 1966. It was one evening in June that year, when a married couple were on a fishing trip with their son, who was a teenager. They were situated at the remote lake and were the only ones there. It was peaceful and quiet and exactly what they were hoping for; until something very disturbing happened.

Suddenly they found themselves engulfed in what they later described as "complete darkness and silence." The darkness came in an instant and was pitch black. The silence was disturbed only by a strange 'grinding' sound and what "smelt like metal burning." They clung to each other for comfort and reassurance but they suddenly realised that they couldn't feel their son. They reached all around for him in the blackness, but could not feel him anywhere, and despite their shouts for him, they received no reply back. He had literally disappeared while standing next to them.

Moments later, the absolute blackness 'evaporated' and their son reappeared as though out of no-where. He was stuttering and told them that he'd seen a 'disk-shaped airplane' and had gone towards it. He could remember nothing after that.

It was reported by his parents, in their letter to the Canadian Ufologist Mr Colombo, that their boy's state of amnesia quickly deteriorated into madness and that they had no choice but to confine him in a psychiatric facility, where he remained permanently.

Long since known for its variety of strange phenomenon including odd experiences of those hiking there, as well as strange lights and 'UFO sightings', anyone going into the woods of Ninham Mountain State Forest, in Carmel, New York State, may find themselves overcome by the feeling of extreme vertigo, hear voices calling to them in strange languages, or suffer bizarre feelings of unreality and unexplained visions.

Perhaps the most interesting incident on record is that of an ex-military intelligence officer who allegedly had the most disturbing of experiences. He was interviewed by Philip Imbrogo and Marianne Horrigan during their extensive investigation into the paranormal characteristics of the area, for their book 'Celtic Mysteries.' The man spoke to them back in 1992 and told them he was very familiar with the area, having camped and hunted there for many years.

The incident itself took place in January of 1992. He said he was walking through the woods until he reached the top of the mountain, where the wind was really strong. He estimated it was 40 below. He began to walk back down through the woods when it began to snow.

Already cold and with the sun now gone down, the temperature began to drop and he said it felt as though his feet and hands were already developing frostbite. It then began snowing very hard and it came down so thick and fast that he couldn't see more than ten feet in front of him. He said he was lost now, and could barely walk. He knew he was still pretty high up, and there were no trees or bushes to shelter him from the wind, since most of the tress were bare. The sky was very dark and the fog was surrounding him. He started losing orientation and had no idea what direction he'd started walking in. He said he felt dizzy and fell down and couldn't move once he was on the floor. He thought he was going to freeze to death up there and be found weeks later, dead. He couldn't feel anything; no pain, but he couldn't move either, he felt frozen already. It was as if all his joints had frozen. As he looked up into the sky right overhead ten or more lights of different colors appeared out of nowhere and started to come down. He heard no sound and the lights were in the shape of a circle. They were strange to see especially because they looked fuzzy through the mist and fog. Then he blacked out. The next thing he remembers was when he woke up in the ranger's station at the bottom of the mountain. The ranger told him he found him at the bottom of the parking area lying down on top of the hood of a car.

Even more bizarre, the man says, "The ranger also told me he received a telephone call saying I was there! - I don't know how I got there; there was no way that I could have walked all that distance alone. Those lights must have been some sort of ufo. They must have been benevolent since they saved me. It seems that from the point I blacked out to the time that I woke up in the station I was missing for about 40 minutes. Whoever they were they didn't keep me for a long period of time. The only thing I remember is being in a room and seeing tall canisters with figures that looked like people in them.

Even more chilling, he says, "I know this sounds crazy, but in the dream I remember seeing a canister that was empty and I really feel that whoever they were they are going to come back for me because that's the canister I'm s'posed to be in."

Ufologist and ex-Navy man, Jorge Martin, in Evidencia OVNI, reported on a strange case that took place in El Yunque rainforest, Puerto Rico. It occurred in 1965, in a place that is rife with the weirdest of inexplicable encounters and experiences. An 8 year old school girl called Maria Figueroa was in the forest with her school class and their teachers, when they suddenly realized she had gone missing. Despite the most intensive of searches utilizing the military, who were based not far from the forest, the police, expert searchers, and trackers, she was never found.

It was only years later that a woman told newspapers of what had happened. She said she had been there that day as a young girl and had heard her school friend scream, and when she had gone to see where the scream was coming from she had seen the little girl trying to wrestle free from two tall men in 'gray-blue coveralls.' They had hold of her friend and wouldn't let her go, she said, and they warned the woman now telling her story that in no uncertain terms was she to tell of what she had witnessed or they would take her too. They told her to run fast, coming forward as though to snatch her, and she fled as fast as she could. She said she had not remembered this until she was older because she had blocked it from her mind until it resurfaced.

Was her memory serving her correctly? Did they seem tall to her because she was only small at the time, or were they unnaturally tall? Were they human, or 'other'?

In Brazil, the strange disappearance of a boy scout gripped the nation and led to one of the greatest mysteries Brazil has known. The case left a mark of fear and uncertainty because to this day no indication of what happened has been discovered. On August 6th, 1985, a small scout group went trekking in the forested mountain region near the city of Picket, Sao Paulo. The group consisted of Juan Cespedes Bernabeu, the scout leader, and four scouts all in their mid-teens. They were Marcus Aurelius Bosaja Simon, Ricardo Salvione, Osvaldo Lobeiro, and Ramatas Rohm. Only three of the four scouts returned.

Marcus Salvione disappeared in a way that would almost seem 'supernatural' when he disappeared without leaving any tracks or trail.

His father, a journalist called Ivo said, "At no time have I considered he is dead," but he also has no idea what happened to him.

While the mountain top reaches as high as 2420 metres above sea level, and is a rocky climb, it can be achieved without the use of specialist climbing equipment. The group had set up camp at the base and were in the process of trekking uphill on one the steep trails.

As the group were ascending the trail, one of the other boys, Osvaldo, slipped and dislocated his knee. Thinking that they may need to summon rescuers with a stretcher, the scout leader asked one of the boys to go back to the base to fetch medical assistance. Marcus volunteered to be the one to head back down to the base, and the scout leader agreed for him to go but told him to leave chalk markers of his route as he went back down. He was to leave markers saying "240" which was the number of their scout group. When the rest of the group got back to base later, having received no medical assistance, they found that the team there did not know of their predicament, as Marcus was not there. It appeared that he had never arrived back at the base.

For the next 28 days, civilian volunteers, the police, and the military went over the region with a fine tooth comb. They searched on foot and with helicopters. They found no body, no pieces of clothing, and just two chalk markings saying "240." There were no more markings after that, and no trace of the boy was found. It was as if Marcus had "evaporated".

The Police and military searched so scrupulously, covering every inch, that a soldier who had lost a knife in the middle of the forest found it the next day while searching again. That's how minute the searching method was in terms of scouring every inch of the forest and mountain. To this day however, Marcus Aurelius has never been seen again, and no clues about his mysterious disappearance have ever emerged.

Once a searcher asked the boys parents if they believed in 'flying saucers' and suggested they go to Brasilia to speak with an Air Force general, who was aware of extraterrestrial phenomena. The General said he could communicate with aliens telepathically. Desperate and willing to do anything to have their son back, his parents told the General to ask the aliens to return their child. They received no response from the General.

The tragedy that shook the family moved the entire country too, with the press and television following the desperate search. For a month, over 300 people including volunteers, fire-fighters and teams specializing in search and rescue had stayed in the forest, scouring the Pico dos Marins region without any success.

The boy's mysterious disappearance and the fact that they completely failed to find any trace of the Boy Scout left everyone who participated in the searches absolutely bewildered, as well as the authorities involved. There found none of his things, such as his knife, or water bottle. Nothing was found. It was like he was never there, and his disappearance remains an enigma to this day.

The scout party had set up base at the property of Afonso Xavier, who himself had five decades of experience as a guide in the area. Even he could find no clues about the boy's disappearance. He had gone with the scouts initially, but when the scout leader realised they could easily make it on their own, he said they could manage without him. The area itself is a common and popular spot for tourists and other hikers heading up to Pico dos Marins, and there was a clear trail to follow.

According to "Operation Marins" written by investigator Rodgrigo Nunes, the last time the scout Simon Marcus Aurelius was seen was at 2.40pm. The rest of the group had passed by two "240" marks made by Marcus, but after that they came to a fork, with tracks left and right. The group believed that Marcus had gone down the path on the left, but that path had obstacles, so that was not going to work for them, because they were carrying Osvaldo supported on their shoulders. The group leader decided to take the trail on the right. The leader later said he thought it would be no problem and that they would cross later and re-join with the trail the boy had taken.

The path they took however became longer than they expected and they didn't make it back to the camp until 5:30 in the morning, taking about 15 hours to accomplish their trek down, all the while carrying the injured boy.

Everyone thought they would find Marcus sleeping in the camp tent, but when they arrived, they found the tent empty with the belongings the boy had brought on the expedition still there, ruling out the possibility that he had made it back and, for some reason, left the base and gone home.

Officers of the Military Police, an Army Infantry Battalion, sniffer dogs, trackers, guides, and even parapsychologists, psychics, and clairvoyants arrived to participate in the efforts. It was one of the greatest searches ever held in the country, but nothing has ever been found.

Some of the assumptions made at the time were initially that the disappearance had to be tied to the scout leader, but he was easily ruled out after the other boys were questioned; he never left them alone at any point during the trek down. Another theory was that the boy could have fallen into a hole, but if this had occurred, the decomposing body would have drawn the attention of the cadaver dogs who participated in the search, and that did not happen. The third hypothesis was that he could have been "abducted" by aliens. The Pico dos Marins is considered 'a region with very strong magnetic power,' which, according to mystics, attracts extraterrestrial craft. Accordingly, the family sought out Ufologists, but they also could not explain what had happened.

"We went to psychics and spiritualists including a famous medium Chico Xavier. Most say that he is alive," says the boy's father.

Xavier told his father, "I only communicate with people who disincarnated, not the living," and so because of this, the family believe the boy is still alive.

The only possible clue came on the second night of the search, when the scout leader and the other scouts were preparing to get some sleep after searching all day. They heard a scream, followed by the sound of a whistle. They were all astonished, as they knew the boy scout wore a whistle, as they all did with their scout uniform.

At the sound of the whistle, everyone ran out of the tent and with the guide Afonso, they headed toward the forest. Suddenly they saw a flash of blue light in the forest, followed by two more flashes.

The group leader, Juan Bernabeu, took hold of his whistle and started to blow it, hoping to hear the boy's whistle again but it didn't come and there was only silence.

That's what made Ufologists say that it was at that moment that the boy was 'taken.' The group reported the incident to the police and military searching for the boy, but they found no source for the blue lights and still no sign of the boy.

Chapter 6:
A case like Dyatlov

In a case that perhaps bears some similarities with the Dyatlov Pass incident, John Cooper & Jeannette Johnson tried to do something very few would attempt; they tried to climb South America's highest mountain during the worst month of the year; but they never made it to the top of Mount Aconcagua, Argentina. Their adventure was cut short by something that has baffled authorities for years.

The macabre mystery began in the summer of 1972. It was then that 8 climbers first got together to discuss scaling the 22,840 foot mountain. There was a lawyer, a doctor; a psychologist; a geologist, a policeman, and a farmer, as well as the couple formerly mentioned, Jeanette a teacher and John Cooper an engineer.

When the group arrived in the tiny town of Mendoza in the Andes to undertake the climb, local experts ominously warned them that January was a bad time of year to do it. The expedition however brushed their concerns aside, but they agreed to hire a local climber Miguel Angel Alfonso as a guide. Miguel told them to wait for better weather, but they were determined to begin as soon as possible, and on a freezing morning the party set out.

At first the climbing progressed relatively steadily, but very quickly several of the group found they were unable to continue in the weather conditions of ice and driving winds. First, two of the party dropped out, urging the others to give up but to no avail. Then one more of the party gave up too and the guide recalls that at this stage, they were 6,300 metres up. The man had mountain sickness and had lost control of his body. The guide took him back to base, leaving just four to continue the expedition.

"That was the last time I saw Jeannette and Cooper alive," the guide says.

"Three days later in the base camp there was a terrible storm and I was looking out of the cabin when I saw two figures in the far distance. Intending to go out and help them, I was forced back by the weather. The following day, I went back out and did succeed in reaching them. They were walking in circles and babbling, crying and blinded by the sunlight. There should have been four but there were only two of them. The two that did return were in a terrible condition from frostbite and they were both incoherent. They began shouting, "Cooper is where the road nears the trees. We're not men, not athletes ... They were ghosts. Jeannette has been taken by the women on mules."

He had no idea what the men were talking about. "The other two never returned. Later that year, another expedition came across the grisly remains of Cooper. There was a strange wound, in his stomach, perhaps caused by an ice-pick. But there were also multiple fractures in his skull and it was those that had killed him."

"It was to be another two years before a subsequent expedition found Jeanette's body, perfectly preserved in ice. She had been brutally beaten. No one has ever been able to find the reason for their deaths, and it seems it will remain a secret kept by the mountain."

Had the two men in their party killed them? How could "women on mules" have been there, up so high on the mountain and in such treacherous conditions? Had the men who said they had seen them been delirious with frostbite and hypothermia and hallucinated them? What did they mean, "They were ghosts?" Who are they referring to?

If it were possible for women to be up there on mules, why would they kill those two climbers and not the other two? Or had someone else killed them? Yet there were no other expeditions at the time they went up the mountain. All other parties had been wise enough not to attempt it in the weather conditions.

What had happened to them and how had they died?

The last time that Cooper had been seen by the other climber Zeller, he was not in the condition in which he was found, in that he was reportedly not fatally injured from a fall or lying down with serious fractures in his skull. The climber had said he had left him 'sitting.' Furthermore, the female climber was found on a section of the mountain where there was virtually no incline, which made it unlikely that she too had fallen. She was also found at quite some distance away from the other climber. Both had sustained multiple fractures yet neither of the other two climbers, who did make it back to base, had said anything about them having a fall or accident, and where they were both found was not consistent geographically with them landing from a fall.

The authorities declared that murder had taken place, implying that Jeanette had killed her companion with an ice pick, and then had a fall. The forensics of the case however do not seem to add up to the geography, and it would appear that the mountain has indeed kept the secrets of their deaths.

Patrick N wrote into Sasquatch Chnonicles, "We'd been canoeing and camping along the lakes between Minnesota and Canada. This day we were going to canoe for a few hours but a storm started to blow and so we got out at a clearing and set up camp quickly to try and avoid the storm.

Next morning it'd cleared up and we started looking for a good fishing spot. We came upon another campsite, however it was completely wrecked. There was trash everywhere, there were clothes on the ground, the tent was torn and had collapsed. At first we were just like disgusted, but the closer we looked, the weirder things were. For one, their food was still tied high up in a tree to keep bears from it, but the bags were literally ripped open; despite being tied at least thirty feet up. Second, literally everything; rope, pans, hiking stuff, clothes, and food was all still there. Half of it was all torn up, half of it had not been touched at all.

We waited around for a few hours and then decided to call the helicopter crew who were to come and get us when we were leaving. We asked them if they'd heard any distress calls but they said they weren't aware of any. We were pretty upset by it. First we thought bear attack; but the food was still there not eaten. Why was half they stuff destroyed and not the other half? And the ripped bags at 30 feet up?"

A bird could reach the bags and rip them open perhaps, but not trash a complete camp surely? So what did the damage? And where were the campers?

David Brewster, writing for Seattle Magazine in August 1970, describes what was possibly a fatal

Sasquatch attack; fatal in that the victim died in fleeing from the creature, or from something in Mount St Helens National Park.

'One of the eeriest encounters with Sasquatch may have occurred here in 1950. A well-known climber, Jim Carter, disappeared. Ski tracks indicated he had careered downward, taking the most risky chances, as one searcher later put it, "that no-one of his calibre would take, unless something was terribly wrong or he was being pursued." In his wild descent, this experienced man jumped several yawning crevices before going right off a steep canyon.'

'Neither he nor his equipment were ever found, and there were several members of the search party who reported that while they were searching they had the unnerving sensation of feeling they were being watched all the time they were there. Among the searchers was Bob Lee, who admitted that both he and some of the Mountain Rescue Council, came to the same conclusion; "The apes got him."

Brewster continues, 'In Indian tales, she (Sasquatch) is a cannibal and the Kwakiutl of Northern Vancouver have a singular theme; she kidnaps children, sometimes by disguising herself as their grandmother, seals up their eyes, and carries them off on her back.'

When the Danish explorer Knud Rasmussen arrived in arctic North America in 1921 to study the Iglulik Eskimos, he found a culture that revolved almost entirely around a multitude of unseen beings; "spirits that inhabited every person, animal and object, and spirits that were held responsible for seemingly inexplicable events, such as illness or bad weather. With the aid of an Eskimo shaman named Anarqaq, who drew for him pictures of the unseen spirits he saw, the explorer learned of invisible entities who were either kind and helpful or malevolent, aggressive, and evil. The Shaman told him that the entire community worked together to try to keep the bad spirits at bay, by practising rituals and taboos, but it seemed that only the shaman himself was able to conqour the spirits and drive them out. Anarqaq said that he was helped in his endeavours by the benevolent spirits who came to his aid. Interestingly, he said that many of these kind spirits would often first appear as monsters or ferocious monsters, but once they were won over they remained steadfast and readily available to him to help him.

Anarqaq held the firm belief that an entity called Igtuk was responsible for the booming noises that were heard coming from arctic mountains. The shaman said he had seen this entity and it had just one huge eye which was set into his body at the same level as his arms. His mouth opened wide to disclose a dark abyss, and he was covered in thick dark hair. In a vision that appeared to the Shaman one spring day, a female spirit named Qungairuvlik tried to steal a child by concealing it in her parka. Before she could accomplish the deed however, two well-armed helping spirits came to the rescue of the child, he said, and killed the kidnapper. One of the many spirits that Anarqaq claimed to have encountered during hunting expeditions was a monstrous being as big as a bear. With a mighty roar, the monster called the Kigutilik rose from an opening in the ice as the shaman was hunting seal. Anarqaq said he was so terrified that he fled without even attempting to try calling any spirit helpers.

With 7 million acres of primeval forest, this national park has no roads and access is usually by air. There's evidence of prehistoric humans being here. The Nahanni Valley in Canada's Northwest Territories has been called one of the few remaining unexplored places in the western world. Much of it remains unchartered, despite it being declared a national park four decades ago.

It's a place where bears and wolves reside, and possibly something else. The Genoskwa too are said to live there. The Genoskwa are a sub-species of the Sasquatch, and in Native American lore are called the 'Giant Stone Men.' They are rumored to be more aggressive than the Sasquatch, and are larger, estimated at between 9 and 11 feet and weighing at least 800 lbs.

In the 18th century, the fur traders came to the region, followed by the gold prospectors. It's the 200 mile gorge where most disappearances are said to have happened. Natives say that is where true evil lurks. It's been given the name of 'The Valley of the Headless Men' for good reason. During the gold rush there were a series unexplained incidents. Two brothers, Will and Frank McLeod seemed to disappear in the valley in 1906. It wasn't until two years later that other prospectors found their bodies. They had been decapitated. A decade passed quietly until another prospector, a Swiss man by the name of Martin Jorgenson was found headless too.

In 1940's, a Canadian gold miner was discovered dead in his sleeping bag. His head too had been removed. That same year a prospector called Ernest Sacabe was found without a head, decapitated.

They were just the ones who were found. In the '60's it was estimated that more than 50 men had gone into the valley and never come back out. Their bodies have never been found.

Here is an old newspaper account of a very grisly, disturbing and perplexing case.

"MAN ON MOUNTAIN SIDE FOR SIX DAYS," reads the headline from the Welsh Newydd Cymru Arlien Newspaper of 14th September, 1907.

The article says, "How the man got into the position in which he was found is enshrouded in mystery, and, although he was breathing when discovered, he was unable to give any account of himself. He had been idle for a week or so owing to a stoppage at a local quarry, and he left home on Thursday in last week for the purpose of seeking employment. It is said he arrived at Pont-neath-Vaughan during the morning of the 5th, but it is not known at what time he left for the return journey, though it is believed it was towards the evening. About half-a-mile from Pont-neath-Vaughan is an embankment, and Jones must have fallen down it. He was found by William and John Jones, who on Wednesday morning had proceeded to search for him. His disappearance was only notified to the police that morning, it being believed that he had secured work some-where away from home. A terrible spectacle met the searchers' eyes as they reached the spot. The man, who was embedded in fern, was still alive, and lifted up his left hand on the approach of his discoverers as if asking them to hasten to his aid. His skull was fractured, and his eyes, face, and that part of his body in contact with the ground had been devoured. It is stated that before he died early on Thursday morning he tried to speak, but his voice had lost all its power.

The report says that the man was "partly undressed," with the "flesh literally picked off his face, and the eyes eaten away. The man was still alive, but died soon after."

It was later said that he must have been eaten by vermin or birds, which is perhaps one possibility...

The Aberdare Leader Newspaper followed up on the poor man's inquest.

"Penderyn Tragedy. An inquest was held by the Coroner (Mr R. W. Jones) at the Lamb Hotel, Penderyn, on Friday afternoon touching the death of David John. Dr. Thomas of Hirwain, said that he was called to deceased about 11 o'clock on Wednesday night. He found him in an unconscious condition. There were bruises on his legs. There were maggots in the cut on his head and also in one of his eyes. The bruises appeared to have been caused by accident. Elizabeth John, the widow of the deceased, who wept bitterly in giving her evidence, said that deceased was 41 years of age and the father of two children. He had left home stating that he was not sure whether he would go to look for work at a quarry or go and work on the hay. He promised to be back that evening. Her husband had been out of work owing to a strike at the quarry. He did not return that night. In the morning she told her neighbours of her husband having not returned home, whereupon they told her to let matters be because he would be sure to return shortly. As he did not return on Sunday and on Monday she went to some men in the village and asked them to go in search of her husband. They declined because they were busy at the time. She did not inform the police until Wednesday. Her husband was brought home on Wednesday evening last and died the following day. The Coroner at this point said that there had been a serious neglect on the part of witness in not having taken steps earlier to find deceased as he had promised to be back on the same night. He sympathised with the widow but she ought to have reported to the police. William Kemys, Pont-neath-vaughan, said that he met the deceased on the 3rd in Pont-neath-vaughan. They went into the White Horse public house together. Witness gave him some beer and some bread and cheese. Deceased told him that he was in search of work. Witness then promised him two or three days' work on his farm if he came up with witness. Deceased refused this offer on the ground that he promised his wife to be home that night. Witness, who was accompanied by Mrs Harris, the landlady of the White Horse, then left the deceased who proceeded to walk towards Penderyn. William Jones, of Green Cottage and Jn. Jones, of Gwalia House, spoke to finding deceased lying amongst some ferns. P.S. Davies said that he went to the place where deceased had been found. He found the clothing strewn about the ground. They also came across a pool of blood among some ferns. The Coroner summed up, and said it was one of the saddest cases he had ever inquired into. According to the two discoverers' story, when John's wife became very anxious as to his whereabouts, they undertook to walk over the mountain from Penderyn in the direction of Pont-Neath-Vaughan. When they reached the Dinas Rock, "on Cilhepste Mountain, they found him. His trousers, boots, and stockings were lying some 50 yards away. When they got in sight the unfortunate man raised his hand as if making a signal for help, but when they reached him he was unable to articulate a word. His body was badly bruised as if by a fall, and there were several deep cuts on the head. His eyes were swollen, but whether they were gone or not is not known. One of the men at once proceeded to the village of Pont-Neath-Vaughan for some brandy and also to Glynneath, for a doctor. Here Dr. Dyke at once accompanied him to the spot where the man lay: and he ordered him to be taken home. On the bank of the river was found a silver watch and chain and a man's hat, stick, and pipe at various points along the bank.'

Quite simply, the poor man most likely suffered a fall, and was then eaten by natural predators; but why were his clothes strewn 50 yards from his body? Why were his heavy work boots and his trousers no longer on his body? Why was his watch found further away by the stream? Why would he have been eaten while still alive? What happened to him out alone there on that terrible night? Was it simply a natural accident and natural predation, or was it something else?

Chapter 7:
Hunted by Humans?

The following letter was recently found in the woods in British Columbia;

"This message is for a certain young lady who has several terriers. I see you nearly every day in here. Every time I see you I want to approach you but I find myself overcome with shyness and jumping off the trail and watching you from afar, but yesterday I slipped up. I was too close and you could smell my cologne. I was close enough to hear you ask your friend if she smelled it. You seem to realize you are being watched. I know that your dog saw me because the hairs on its back stood up. I am very impressed every time I see you in the woods. Perhaps the bear spray and concealed knife I know you carry give you a sense of security. I realise others may find this creepy...'

The January 17 2014 issue of the The Times Colonist displayed the very creepy letter found in the woods on Beaver Lodge trail in Campbell River, British Columbia. The police had requested it be released as a warning.

The writer of the letter ends by saying that he doesn't mean to scare her, that he just wants to say hello! The police are now looking for him, and have warned women to be careful when going into the woods as they are not sure what the unidentified man is capable of.

Daisey writes on Websleuths forum,

"My son was an avid hiker during college. His dream was to hike the Appalachian Trail. When he took off alone he had plans to meet up with other hikers at various points so none of them would be hiking alone too long. Two weeks into his trip, he called me to pick him up after getting an injury in a fall. Turns out he left camp in the middle of the night and was injured trying to evade several guys that had been stalking him for days."

'Anonymous' posts on a hiking forum, about an experience while hiking in Georgia, "It involved my hiking partner and I being followed. We had a scary experience one time on one of the trails. My hiking partner and I were being very closely followed and we were very frightened by these men. I believe we were saved only when we spotted other hikers and shouted out "Hey, here's some more hikers," because the men following us then took off up the hillside."

The Hour Newspaper reported on a case in November 1989, of a mid-twenties female student who'd got lost for two weeks in the wilderness of South Carolina, in Table Rock National Park.

She was found by a hunter, but what she told the authorities who'd been searching for her for a week with a party of over one hundred people, was quite alarming.

She said that she'd run off the main trail and into the woods when she sensed that she was being pursued by a group of men who she thought meant to do harm to her.

"There was no good intent involved," she told reporters.

Although she could see the search helicopters overhead, she said that she had been too frightened to create a fire to alert them because she believed if she had done so, then the men stalking her would also have been able to find where she was.

The authorities didn't believe her.

"From the very start, before the search was initiated she became paranoid that somebody was trying to run her down," said Walter Purcell of Emergency Preparedness in the county.

"We don't think anybody was chasing her," the deputy Sheriff commented.

The consensus of belief was that they think she saw hunters and panicked, thinking that they were after her, and that she then thought the rescuers were the same men too, hunting her.

Surely hunters look different to S&R teams?

Perhaps the authorities were right not to believe her. After all, they were probably irritated that they'd just spent exhausting and intensive man-hours over the period of week trying to find her.

Had she made the story up out of embarrassment because she'd caused everyone to come out searching for her after she'd accidentally got lost? Possibly, but the statement she made to the Press was very clear. She could tell that 'there was evil intent.'

Perhaps they were right to say that they didn't believe any men were chasing her and that there was no evidence to support this, given that they'd been covering the same ground looking for her; however if they couldn't find her for seven days because she managed to evade and elude them, wouldn't the men who were allegedly chasing her also have been able to evade and elude the searchers?

Eloise Lindsay herself was sure there were men stalking her.

Said to be one of the most intriguing and perplexing of mysteries in recent years, and one that has had thousands of people tying to figure out just what may have happened, is the vanishing of student Maura Murray.

A hard working student nurse at Amherst University, she had a busy schedule of attending lectures, doing nursing practice, and she had two jobs. She had a fiancé out of State and a Father who frequently visited her, and much of her childhood had been spent hiking with him in the countryside.

She had a security job at the dormitories and she been at her post there when she'd had received a telephone call that had upset her. Her supervisor even had to escort her back to her room because she was too upset to continue working that night.

What isn't known is who called her and what it was they said to her.

The next day she inexplicably invented a death in the family to use as an excuse to tell to her teachers, explaining that she had to leave college for a few days to get back for the funeral; but there had been no death.

After sending emails to her lecturers, she packed up some of her things, including some pictures from her wall, and about a week's worth of clothing, her gym kit, jewellery her fiancé had given her, and some of her study books.

She also took some alcohol, a book about true stories of hiking in the Mountains, and directions to get to Vermont.

Then she got into her car and drove off, but she crashed her car outside of Woodsville in New Hampshire. It was February of 2004 and it was a cold night.

She didn't seem to be hurt when a coach driver passed and stopped to see if she was ok, but he asked if she needed him to call the police. She said she didn't because she had already done so, but it seems he doubted her story because he knew that cell phone coverage was poor in that area and so, still concerned, when he reached his house only a minute or so beyond the crash site, he called them anyway.

The police arrived only minutes later and found the car was locked but she wasn't inside and they couldn't see her anywhere.

The front window was cracked and the air bags had deployed during the crash. The police were concerned for her well-being and after an initial search of the area they escalated the incident and instigated a full-blown search for the now missing girl.

Soon helicopters were flying overhead looking for her.

Her Father and her boyfriend were informed that they could not locate her.

Her boyfriend left Oklahoma to travel up and as he was travelling he received a voicemail message to his phone that came from a pre-paid calling card. He could only hear breathing and then crying, but he believes it was his fiancée.

The problem was that she hadn't told anyone where she was heading. Earlier that day, she had withdrawn most of her money, which was less than $500, and phoned a condo rental in another part of New Hampshire, but hadn't booked a rental.

She'd also stopped on her drive that night to buy some alcohol and when the police assessed the crash scene they believed that they found traces of spilt wine.

Had she fled the scene through fear of getting a DUI?

If she had, where had she gone on that cold night? Though she was used to hiking growing up, this was late at night and winter and she'd been drinking, which would only make her feel colder if she was outside.

Among the theories put forward over the years are that she fled for the Canadian border for some reason; or that she was taken by a serial killer who monitored the police scanners to get a lead on potential victims. Others think she ran and hid from the police and suffered hypothermia and died.

But if she had died out there off the route, why couldn't even the cadaver dogs find her body? The police didn't find any tracks from the road into the woodland around the road.

How long could she have survived a new life without any money in her account, and no-where to go? Why would she leave her fiancé and Dad? It didn't make sense to them at all; and she'd packed her study books; indicating that she was intending to use them, and not leaving her old life behind.

Had someone taken her against her will? She'd spent three months as a cadet at West Point Naval Academy before transferring college and knew how to look after herself, but she had been in an emotional state and drinking that night. Then again, someone with a gun on a dark night could have taken her at will.

To this day, no word has been heard from her still. Maura Murray is still missing. It's possible she hid out in the woods, afraid of being arrested, but if she did, why couldn't the searchers find her? And why didn't she come out from where she was hiding after the police had left?

Another very strange case is that of Tara Calico and a young boy. In 1998, Tara Calico was a busy young woman. She worked at a bank in town, was studying for a degree in psychology, and fitted around this she regularly worked out or participated in sports.

She often went out for bike rides, and that day as she set out on her usual morning ride, she asked her Mom to look out for her when it got to midday, and if she wasn't back by then she wanted her Mom to come and pick her up. She was concerned because in the past she'd got a puncture on her bike and been delayed and she had a lot to do that day.

When midday came and went and her daughter didn't return home, her Mom duly set out in her car to go find her and bring her and the bicycle back home. But when she drove along the route her daughter always took, she didn't see her at all. Checking all the way, she then returned back home but her daughter still wasn't there and now concerned she immediately called the police.

A patrol car quickly arrived and started searching for her and the police found a cassette tape along the road that looked like it had probably come out of her

Walkman stereo, but no other signs of her or the bicycle, just some bike tracks.

Where she was cycling was a straight route that cut through in a straight line, with very few cross sections, no buildings and no trees. There wasn't really anywhere for her to be if she wasn't on the road.

As the police extended their search area to a distance of nearly twenty miles away they came across a walkman lying in the road that her Mother identified as hers. She believed then that her daughter was trying to leave them clues and a trail to follow. This was close to a remote Campground called John F Kennedy. The trail ended there, at the base of the Mazano Mountain.

Witnesses had last seen her at close to noon, and less than two miles from her home. They'd also seen a pickup truck close behind her. The police were never able to trace the truck.

A year passed with no further leads or information or clues about the girl's disappearance. Despite the police searching everywhere for her, no other signs could be found and they were at a complete loss to explain what had happened to her.

Then, a year later and hundreds of miles away in a parking lot outside of a grocery store in Florida, a lady parked her car and walked into the store. When she returned, the white truck that had been parked next to hers was now gone, but what she found in the parking space on the floor was something terrible.

It was a Polaroid picture with a harrowing scene. Two children were lying on a bed, bound and gagged. A boy who looked to be in early adolescence, and an older girl. They were both staring into the camera anxious and scared and the image horrified the woman.

The woman drove quickly to the nearest police station, telling them that it must have been dropped by the man she had seen in the driver's seat; a man with dark hair and a moustache.

The police responded immediately, setting up road blocks to try to find him but it was too late and he'd already left the area.

When the mother of missing Tara was shown the picture, she was convinced it was her daughter. The parents and family of a missing boy were convinced the boy in the picture was their son too. He also went missing in New Mexico the same year. He'd been at a campsite in the Cibola National Park in the Zuni Mountains, less than fifty miles from where the girl lived. He had gone with his Dad and a friend of his Father to hunt turkeys.

They had only been at the campsite for a short while and were still setting up when they realised that young Michael had disappeared. They quickly started looking for him, thinking he must have gone off wandering but they couldn't see him anywhere nearby and quickly found a ranger and reported him missing.

The search was started but a sudden storm came and made it extremely difficult to look for him in the wilderness. Snow was falling fast despite it having been quite warm earlier in the day and the child had only thin clothing on. Nearly five hundred people searched for him, including the Rangers, the National Guard, the police and many volunteers, spanning out over a ten mile radius of the site. Even air searches were carried out.

Tracks thought to be his were seen in the snow but no-one could be absolutely sure they were his. Despite bloodhounds being used, there were just too many other scents from all of the volunteers and SAR teams, making it impossible for the dogs to distinguish the boy's scent.

Despite a week long search, the little boy was not found. What most involved believed had happened was that he must have wandered off, become quickly lost and disoriented, having only just arrived in the area and being completely unfamiliar with it, and become unable to find his way back to the camp ground.

Most of those involved in the search believed that what had happened to him was that he had then succumbed to the cold and died of exposure and eventually his body would have suffered natural predation. They also felt that when hypothermia began to set in and became severe he would possibly have burrowed and crawled into an enclosed area, which was what victims often did according to their years of search experience.

But still no remains were found.

And then came the Polaroid photograph, which both families said contained the bound images of their children. The boy's Father said at the time that even the boy's best friend said it was definitely the boy. Although the Father said he wasn't sure, he also didn't know if that was because he didn't want to accept that it was his child pictured in so vulnerable a position.

But then there was a new twist in 1990. The boy's remains were discovered approximately eight miles from the campground in the mountains. A horse rider had come across some human bones in a thick copse of trees that were identified as him. No-one could explain how he had ended up dead eight miles away.

It now seemed unlikely that the boy had been taken to Florida and then returned to the mountain.

But if it wasn't Michael, then who was the other boy in the photograph?

Between then and now, two other photographs were reported as possibly containing the missing girl.

They were never released to the press or the public but it's known that one photo is an out of focus image of a girl with duct tape over her mouth, mysteriously found at a construction site. It was examined and it was discovered that the type of film was only manufactured after 1989. The second photograph was of a woman on a train, blindfolded.

Neither were positively identified as the missing girl nor were they ruled out either. Her Mom felt that it could be her, believing the images bore a striking resemblance.

Rivera, the local sheriff said that after twenty years, he was convinced some local boys, whose names he knows, had run her off the road and buried her, probably killing her by accident and then panicked and covered it up. He said that what he lacked however was a solid piece of evidence with which to prosecute them.

However, adding another twist to the mystery again was another photograph that materialised; sent to the police and the local newspapers in 2009, in which there is a young boy who has had a black pen drawn over his mouth, making it look as though his mouth has been gagged, just like in the original Polaroid photo from twenty years ago. Then there is a second photo of the original boy from 1989.

They were sent to the police and media around the time of the anniversary of when Tara went missing. Was it some kind of clue? What was the sender hoping to achieve by sending them? Was it some kind of sick hoax? But if so, how did the sender of them have the original picture of the boy? Was the abductor and possible murderer taunting the authorities, showing them that he'd got away with it?

There was nothing the authorities could do with the photos. There was nothing that would lead to helping them solve the case.

The letters containing the copies of the picture were posted in Albuquerque. The authorities were not sure if the boy in the new photograph was the same as the boy in the original photograph with Tara.

Again, there were no clear answers.

Chapter 8:
Taken, Held, and Drowned

This chapter concerns the rising number of young men who, for the last seven or so years, have disappeared in what can only be described as sinister and inexplicable circumstances. First mentioned in this author's 'Mysterious things in the Woods,' and continued in the books, 'Something in the Woods,' and 'Taken in the Woods,' it refers to the strange and disturbing phenomenon of scores of young men who have been vanishing without a trace, only for many of them to be found dead, weeks or months later, in remote rivers or creeks, shallow ponds or canals, in areas that search parties have thoroughly searched several times before, and their bodies then discovered as though placed there to be found.

As a quick recap before covering new cases, the strange deaths at first were given the meme 'The Smiley Face Killers,' when it was discovered that some of the locations had smiley face graffiti nearby. While this name continues to be used by some, the name has generally been ruled out as being a clue to the reason for any of the missing boys' disappearances and deaths.

Up to 300 young men, predominately in the Midwest, but State-wide, have completely disappeared or been found later, drowned, all under very similar circumstances, and all being of the same demographic victimology. Investigative Journalist Kristi Piehl was the first to publicize the cases back in 2008, through linking up with two detectives who had already discovered the rising number of young college-age men's deaths. Unknown to Piehl, at the same time as she was investigating one strange death, Kevin Gannon and Anthony Duarte, retired NYPD detectives, were already investigating the mysterious deaths of several college men from New York State.

Each of the deaths had been ruled as accidental drowning; then they learned of more student male drowning deaths in the Midwest. In all, the two detectives were able to connect unexplained drowning deaths of at least 40 male students across the whole country. The two detectives came to believe that in each of these cases, there was the possibility that the missing men had been drugged, and their bodies then placed in water, in order to make it appear as if they had drowned.

The two detectives were of the opinion that these deaths were highly likely to be the work of more than one killer, because some of them had taken place on the same day, in separate geographical states. Speaking to CNN, Gannon said, "I believe these young men are being abducted by individuals, taken out, and held for a period of time before they're entered into the water." He stated that he believed the victims were being mentally abused and sometimes physically abused, prior to being killed, though strangely, they usually had no marks on their bodies.

Both Senator Sensenbrenner of Wisconsin and U.S. Congressman McNulty of NY, submitted requests to the FBI for them to investigate the mounting number of disturbing cases occurring and to make efforts to stop them. Instead, the cases have continued and show no signs of abating.

The victim type is always the same; athletic, popular, high achieving white male college students who go missing after a night out drinking with friends. Choosing to go home alone, instead of walking back with friends, they disappear, only to be found some time later, drowned in nearby rivers or creeks.

Many will say they were simply drunk and disoriented and fell in the river. Many will say inevitably, that the reason they are all of a similar victimology is because more young men than women choose to walk off alone at night. They say that they are popular college kids who are letting off steam, drinking too much and then underestimating how much they have drunk, and as a result they then get into difficulty walking home. Others however will ask why they would choose to walk away from their direct route home, often for a long distance, to a remote river or creek, usually in the mid of winter, without coats, and go for a swim or 'fall in,' rather than go straight home? This is the same scenario for almost all of the victims. The majority of them were former lifeguards or very active sportsmen and active outdoorsmen; and most of them were not known to be particularly heavy drinkers. They were all highly intelligent, and understandably not prone to jumping onto rivers and lakes in freezing temperatures, on their own, late at night.

To the detectives and to Piehl, it didn't make sense. Nor did it make sense to some forensic examiners. For the families, who knew their sons the best, the possibility of them drowning was something they found highly unlikely. The detectives, Piehl, many independent pathologists, and the families of the victims all disagreed that the young men had merely fallen prey to the outdoors and misadventure. Piehl and the detectives veered toward a much more sinister explanation; that a group of killers, identities yet unknown, were deliberately targeting these men, for reasons also as yet unknown. And it hasn't stopped.

Detective Gannon and Professor Gilbertson, a nationally acclaimed criminologist based at St Cloud University, Minnesota, were featured on News Channels in the early days of the investigation but Gannon was later accused of allegedly 'inappropriate behaviour' while investigating witnesses and this has probably not helped in furthering the credibility of their investigations. While the mainstream media have largely dismissed the cases as simple 'drinking & drowning deaths' Gretchen Carlson of FOX News presented a documentary on the cases called 'Death at the Rivers Edge,' in August 2014.

Professor Gilbertson, Associate Professor of Criminal Justice, and involved in the organisation 'Nationwide Investigations,' as quoted by NBC, says, "This is a nationwide organization." I spoke to Professor Gilbertson 18 months ago, who at the time pointed out to me that he was concerned that the deaths appeared to have spread to the U.K.

I also spoke at the time with former federal drug enforcement agent Jerry Snyder's organization, a not-for-profit victim-search group called Find Me, composed of active and retired law enforcement officials and consultants. They too had been following the cases from the beginning, and are still investigating them now. "Look at all the names here and we think we've only scratched the surface; that's what's really scary to me,' Snyder said. I had also spoken with several family members of the victims, who were not of the opinion that these were 'accidents.'

Mystery enshrouds so many of these cases and on a side note, while I was looking into these deaths over the last couple of years, I was contacted by a woman who had a blog dedicated to charting and investigating these deaths. At her own request she has asked for anonymity, and while she gave me full access to the records of her blog if I desired, she also warned me that she had been forced to close it down after, in her words, "coming under extreme psychic attack," while running the blog and investigating the deaths, so bad she said, that she now wanted nothing more to do with the investigation. How does psychic astral attack come into this? Who would be behind doing something like that? And why?

She's not the first one to tell me they had been 'forced' to stop looking into things. Another man actively researching the deaths, JC Smith, has also told me of being 'warned off,' and being told 'something similar' to what happened to the victims could happen to him. Additionally, although Kristi Piehl appeared on Coast to Coast am a couple of times in an attempt to bring light to the mysterious events, it was not long afterward that she too closed down her blog about the deaths and refused to have any involvement in the cases. She also lost her job as an investigative reporter, though of course it's not known whether this had anything to do with her active investigations; but there are warning signs that keep flagging up for those who attempt to look into it, and this alone causes me to wonder why.

For those interested in learning more and following the continuing, mysterious, perplexing and possibly very sinister cases of missing college men who are being found later dead in rivers, creeks and even shallow ponds, there is an excellent blog, created several years ago by some of the concerned parents, called 'footprints at the river's edge.' It has very significant details of many of the cases. There is also an investigator called Vance Holmes, who runs the blog 'Drowning in Coincidence,' and who has been following these sinister cases from the very beginning, and again has much detailed information on his blog. There is also the very informative 'killing killers blog' too, run by crime investigator and writer Eponymous Rox.

Are all these people wrong in believing something bad is going on?

When Kristi Piehl first appeared on Coast to Coast radio back in 2008, she was joined by forensic pathologist Dr Michael Sikirica to discuss the tragic case of one of the victims, Todd Geib.

As already covered in my *Something in the Woods* book, in Casnovia, Michigan, 22 year old Todd was last seen at a bonfire party in June 2005. It was a marshy rural area. He left the party to walk back alone to his cousin's house, where he lived. He never made it back there. He had called a friend at 12:51 a.m., but all he had said was, "I'm in a field," before the phone call cut off. When the friend rang back, he answered but all the friend could hear was what sounded like the wind.

The area where he was last seen was thoroughly searched three times. During one of the searches, as many as 1,500 volunteers searched the area. Nothing was found. When his body was discovered three weeks later in a remote bed of water, his death was ruled as drowning; however when a new autopsy was carried out, he was discovered to have been dead only 2-5 days, despite being missing for 3 weeks. In other words, he had been somewhere, alive, for approximately two and a half weeks prior to his death. Where he was found had been thoroughly searched at least 3 times.

When the independent pathologist Dr Sikirica was allowed access to the autopsy files, he concluded through forensic analysis that Todd had been dead only between two to five days; and most crucially, he had no water in his lungs; *he could not have drowned,* and his body was not in the condition it would be expected to be in. He had not been in the water for the twenty or so days he had been missing; meaning that he had been held or kept alive somewhere for approximately three weeks, before being taken to the creek.

Dr Sikirica's opinion was backed up by around 200 other examiners, when he presented the case at an international convention of Medical Examiners.

Piehl said of the cases, "A lot of people have asked me, who is doing this? Whoever had Todd, is a sick individual. I think we're going to find a dark human being, of a kind we haven't met yet," said Piehl.

Recapping another case previously covered in my earlier books, Patrick McNeill was the case that first got the attention of the detectives who found the disturbing pattern. He was 21 when he walked out of a bar in New York City on a cold night in February 1997. He told his friends he was taking the subway back to Fordham University. His body was found near a Brooklyn pier nearly two months later. The Pathologist stated he was not drunk when he died of drowning, and two big questions arose. How did he end up dead in the water in Brooklyn? And where had he been for the last two months?

At his inquest, the Pathologist stated he was not drunk but he died of drowning. Another renowned independent Forensic Pathologist Dr. Cyril Wecht however, when reviewing the case for Kristie Piehl, stated, "There's no way this man is accidentally going to fall into a body of water, (and) the fly larvae (found) have been laid in the groin area. It's an indoor fly—not an outdoor fly. So we have a body that was already dead before it was placed in the water...I would call it a homicide, yes."

In other words, the young man had been kept alive for an extended period of time again, prior to being found in the water; long enough for indoor larvae to settle on his body. He had been kept alive somewhere. Kevin Gannon, investigating the McNeill case since

1997, said, "He was stalked, abducted, held for an extended period of time, murdered, and disposed."

Quickly recapping a couple more of the cases already featured in my earlier books before getting to new ones, Chris Jenkins was a very popular student at the University of Minnesota, and he was on the college swim team. He disappeared one night in 2003. When his body was discovered in the Mississippi river four months after he had disappeared, to the police his death looked like an accidental fall after a night of drinking; however, rather disturbingly, his body was found encased in ice, with his hands folded over his chest, in a manner that is wholly inconsistent with the official verdict of drowning. People drowning do not end up in this position. After justified protest from his family, his cause of death was eventually re-determined as a homicide.

Tyler Blalock, 19, was found in Kraut Creek, on Sept. 29, 2012, in the rural Appalachian State University's southeast side of campus, with police saying it looked like he hit his head and fell in. His mother however, could not understand how her son, a lifeguard, could end up dead in a creek in a cold month.

Honour student Jared Dion, again, like the other boys, a popular and athletic person, was discovered, five days after he disappeared, in the river near Wisconsin University in 2004. At a later autopsy, it was found that he had been moved ten hours prior to his death, and that because his body was still in rigor, he could not have been dead any longer than 72 hours, meaning he had been alive for some time prior to his death and had not died the day of his disappearance. That left 2 days unaccounted for, which again implied that he had been kept somewhere and placed in the water later.

Chillingly Piehl & the detectives found over 100 similar victims; Professor Gilbertson found 300; all young men, all very intelligent and high achievers, all actively fit and often even on the Swim Team. Some will say they were drunk and fell in the water, but for anyone looking into the cases and their autopsies, it's hard to believe this is what really happened.

Professor Gilbertson, talking about one of the cases, has stated that the victim's blood was completely drained from his body prior to him being found.

The two detectives think it's got to be more than one killer. Bodies have been found in different States at the same time.

Is it a gang of serial killers? A syndicate of some kind? A cult? An organised group of some kind that has criss-crossed America, travelling to rural college campuses in 25 different cities in a dozen different states in an ever increasing murder spree?

It's fair to say that young men are prone to misadventure after drinking, and there are tragically many documented cases of drowning worldwide; however, they are not usually found in this number or in these particular ways. It would almost seem as though the men are being deliberately targeted. It is hard to believe that so many educated and sporty men would choose to walk way off their usual route, toward rivers, in the winter, alone, and jump in, or fall in.

Why are the bodies returned to the area previously searched? Is it abductor/abductors? Or is it something less easy to define?

Is this all mere speculation, when the deaths could all be a combination of drink and inevitable accidents?

Some have commented that the victims clothes have been tampered with prior to being found, sometimes being put back on their bodies the wrong way, suggesting that they were removed by someone. Others have said that victims are being recovered with their clothes, wallets, and college ID cards, but that any religious necklaces, such as Crosses and St Christopher' they were wearing, were not recovered.

There are several theories being put forward by many interested in the cases, one of which points to the possibility of their deaths being ritual sacrifices, thought to be based on the ancient alchemy ritual of 'Killing of the Kings,' where the victim's life-force energy is said to be passed to the occult murder(s) at the moment of death, supposedly giving them greater power.

In alchemy ritual a solid substance is said to be 'disolved' in water in a 'slow and silent operation.'

Could this really be what is happening? Is some kind of elite group conducting ancient rituals to further enhance their desire for power, as described in more detail in my previous books when discussing the James Downard theory and the Killing of the Kings, and the 'occult line of tragedy,' in connection with the Jamison family water tower and the Elisa Lam water tower deaths?

Or, is this the work of a serial killer, or is it more likely that it's the work of some kind of organized gang? This is the belief of gang stalking expert Professor Gilbertson? That is his opinion, based on thorough scrutiny of the individual cases, the identical victim type, and what he believes is their abduction, confinement and subsequent death by drowning. But, why death by drowning? Why this particular method of killing?

What type of organized gang would be doing this? A group of travelling and highly organised serial killers? A weird fraternity-related cult? A fanatical religious or satanic group? An MK Ultra-style set up? An elite faction at the lower echelons of the illuminati?

And what is their purpose?

One link that really stands out, as previously discussed in my '*Taken in the Woods*' book, is that very often the young men who go missing have been kicked out of clubs and bars and left to wander the streets often without the means of getting home. Often their coats have been left inside the bars, with their keys and wallets inside. There is also very often the common factor that they have been talking on their cell phones when their calls have suddenly been cut off.

With reference to the victim's being kicked out of the bars, is this a case of negligence of duty of care in the case of doormen? Or is there something more sinister going on in terms of collusion and cooperation between them and the as yet unknown and unidentified gang allegedly stalking and abducting these men?

In several cases afterward, it has been found that although the young men were kicked out, there was no evidence of them causing a disturbance or fight, or even being that drunk. In other words, there was no real reason to throw them out. A reason seems to have been *created*.

As previously described in my other book as a clear example, take the case of Shane Montgomery, a student at West Chester who was escorted out of a Bar in Manayunk, PA, on Thanksgiving 2014, after accidentally tripping into the dj deck.

His body was found 5 weeks later in a part of the river close to the bar where search divers had thoroughly and repeatedly searched. The implication here then being that he was not in the river for all of the time that he had been missing. He was also found in water just three to four feet deep, which would seem a little shallow to drown in surely? Unusually in this case, the FBI quickly became involved in the investigation searching for him, and some have asked why they got involved.

Curiously, it has since been reported that the bar involved stated that there was no disturbance inside the bar and he was not escorted out.

And the other case, in March 2006 when an Ohio med student was having drinks with friends to celebrate spring break. During the evening he called his girlfriend to tell her he was looking forward to the trip they were going to take in a couple of day's time.

In the bar he was seen on the security camera at the top of the elevator, but then he moves out of shot. That was the last time he was seen. An emergency exit was covered by camera; he was not picked up on that either.

The only other route would have been to walk through an area of new construction, although tracker dogs did not detect his scent on searching that area. He has still not been found. Brian Shaffer seems almost to have vanished from inside a bar. Despite there being 3 surveillance cameras capturing all people entering and leaving the bar, he was not seen leaving.

Observers have suggested, 'Something else took him right in that bar.'

As also mentioned in 'Taken in the Woods,' in another case, in February 2015, the distraught parents of a young man went to the Newspapers to speak out about their distress, caused by having to endure listening to their son screaming down the phone to them one night in the last moments of his life.

Holding their phone to another phone which was connected to the emergency services operator, they were begging for help to find where there son was and what was going on.

Their son's last moments of life were heard by the emergency dispatcher but not recorded, contrary to standard operating procedure, due to the recording equipment not working.

The officer later resigned over the matter, upset that it had added to the parents distress. The parents do not feel that the subsequent disappearance of their son was investigated to the extent to which they would have found acceptable.

The police say they are still trying to piece together what might have happened to him, his body having been discovered dead in the Ship Canal three weeks later.

The 21 year old student and volunteer Civic Centre worker had been on a night out with friends. He was last seen at a music event at a racetrack in Manchester city centre, England.

In the early hours of the next morning, his parents were concerned that he had not come home and called him.

His Mother told reporters, "We rang him and when he answered he was incoherent. I could barely make out what he was saying. There was no noise in the background and it struck me that he was on his own. Minutes into the call he started screaming. He was howling and yelling. It was horrific."

While she called the police, her husband took over the phone. He was still screaming.

"It was a howl. I raised my voice at him to try to get him to snap out of it, but I couldn't get through to him. Then suddenly there was silence. There was a total silence, and it was so eerie."

The problem was that they couldn't really do anything because they couldn't find out from him where he was; they couldn't go to his aid.

That phone call was the last anyone heard from him. He was found dead three weeks later in the Canal.

It was later suggested that David Plunkett had been asked to leave the music event, where all alcohol had been free, for being inebriated. Indeed the coroner then wrote to the event organisers, admonishing them for simply evicting someone from an event which they were responsible for, rather then ensuring a duty of care was provided to someone if they became drunk.

When the police tracked his mobile phone records later, it was determined that he'd been a couple of miles outside of the City centre, not near the canals.

At the inquest, the police dispatcher who took the call from the parents described her own trauma from the night's events.

"I took a very distressing 999 call. He was in a distressed state but his parents couldn't hear anything other than his screaming. I stayed on with them for well over an hour, trying to provide assistance for them and him. The incident haunts me still and with each and every new death I see in the news I am more and more convinced that these are not accidents; these are murders."

The death was classified as accidental drowning. His parents clearly disagree with this verdict. They know only too well that he was terrified of something so horrifying he could not even articulate it to them. Whatever he saw was so chilling he could not find the words.

His mother, a former Head Teacher, spoke out, "It is not a case of 'young man drinks too much, falls in canal.' Someone is responsible for his death and the version of events that have been given are simply not adding up, and the case leaves many more questions than answers. He could have been attacked, he could have had his drink spiked; anything.."

This next case in the U.S., again also previously mentioned, bears similarities. Student Daniel Zamlen was reported as a missing person on April 5th 2009. He'd been at a party but his friends who were at the party said that he had left on his own to meet up with another friend at Minnesota University.

They say he was talking with them on his cell phone and was near the Mississippi River Boulevard and St Clair Avenue. Quickly bloodhounds, a helicopter and searchers covered the area where he had been walking, but found no trace of him.

Bloodhounds seemed to get partial hits on his scent near the river, but his father maintains that they kept stopping in the same place, and did but did not actually go near the river. He also said that his own job was as an open pit miner and he understood land, and when he walked that area, he did not believe that someone could just accidently slip into the water there; but if they did, he said it would have left marks and none were found.

In what is one of the most disturbing phone calls, reminiscent of the call received by the parents in Manchester, his friend Anna says she was talking to him when he began to become distressed. By then she says she had left the party and got in her car to go and find him.

'It took a really bad turn,' she told newspapers at the time, "Where are you?" she asked him.

"Oh, my gosh, Help!" – "This was the last thing I heard," she says. "His voice became distant as he said those words, as though he was moving away his phone, and then the line went dead."

She called him back but it just remained unanswered she claims.

It has to be said, his parents have spoken out about the accuracy of statements made by his friends, particularly disputing the content of his last known call.

Disturbingly his Mother also reported that there's significant evidence the drinks at the party had been spiked.

His body was found a month later in the river. A baseball was found near the scene with a smiley face on it, as well as a sign that was marked with smiley face graffiti near the edge.

It was discovered that some of the drinks at the party had been laced with the drug GHB.

His mother has stated "Victims of drowning usually surface within six and ten days after the drowning. The River was flowing four hundred times faster than normal yet Dan's body didn't surface for another 27 days and flowed only two miles."

She says, "The Coroner could not determine 100% that he did drown; just that that was where he was found."

Crucially, she also reports that the night before he disappeared, he was at a Club in the centre of town. He was thrown out because he was not wearing the right wristband.

She says, "He was separated from his friends and later he told his friends that he was approached by men outside. He said that he "ran" from these people. Sound familiar? Maybe he was supposed to have his 'tragic accident' that night, but even though "very intoxicated" he was able to out run these people."

In another bizarre case, college student Mike Knoll was celebrating his birthday with friends in a bar in Wisconsin. It was November 2002 and just after 11.30pm when he walked out of the Bar. He'd been drinking but he wasn't thought by his friends to have been drunk, but for some indefinable reason he wandered into an old lady's home.

She asked him what he was doing and he quickly left her house; but one has to wonder, if he wasn't drunk when he left, how did he manage to become so confused and disoriented as to enter a person's home that he did not know, when he lived in college dorms?

When someone becomes suddenly confused and disoriented it's easy to blame drink but if that's the case why wasn't he like that in the Bar, before he left? Thoughts could then turn to the possibility of drugs being involved, but none of his friends knew him to be a drug taker. Were drugs somehow slipped in his drink perhaps? Or did he encounter someone after he left?

His body was found four months later in the frozen Half Moon Lake. He was half in and half out of the water, which in itself seems highly strange. Where had he been in all those months? The lake had been searched thoroughly several times when he disappeared. His body had no sign of injury. The location was no-where near where he lived or where he had been drinking.

Also mentioned in 'Taken in the Woods,' there was a similar case again in Manchester, England, in June 2012. Chris Brahmy had been to a rock concert on the outskirts of Manchester with a group of friends and after it finished he decided to go into the City Centre to retrieve a new pair of trainers he'd hidden earlier in a car park rather than carry then at the concert all night.

CCTV this time captures over ten minutes of his journey, from retrieving the trainers in a shopping bag to carrying them through street after street in the city centre.

He can clearly be watched walking in a perfectly capable and coherent manner through the streets from around 1.45am until the last CCTV camera films him walking through a passage.

He is not stumbling or wandering around without co-ordination. In other words, he does not appear at all inebriated or under the influence of drugs.

Ten days later, his body is found in the Canal. What the police still do not know is how he ended up in the canal, which at the spot where he was thought to have entered the water, is a high railing that would have required climbing.

"While CCTV follows his movements, we still cannot say how or why he died," the police said.

The spot in which he died was not covered by CCTV. The police also made it clear they had no evidence leading it to be considered suspicious, despite the fact that the coroner found him to have a fractured cheekbone, bruising and cuts to his face.

There were traces of alcohol in his body, and indeed the drug MDMA. Clearly, one could argue the drug caused him to climb up the fence, and jump over it into the canal, although it does beg the question how he managed to find his shoes and walk so capably through the city centre for quite some time without any signs at all of being influenced and made incapable by a drug? Did he encounter someone in the canal area who offered him the drug? Did the drug then make him jump into the canal? Or was he placed into the canal?

Interestingly, the forensic pathologist Ms Carter stated that because the injuries he had sustained had no bruising, they would have happened *after* his death not prior to his death.

In other words, this ruling would imply that he died or was killed without these injuries, then suffered the injuries afterwards. He didn't experience the injuries as a result of throwing himself in the water in a desire to commit suicide. And if the injuries occurred after death, he didn't not inflict them himself.

When I was talking to Professor Gilbertson, he raised concerns that the unexplained phenomenon of identikit young men ending up dead seemed to have spread to England too. Professor Gary Jackson, head of Psychology at the University of Birmingham, England has also officially joined the growing number of people who are perturbed, alarmed, and feel there is something more sinister at play than accidental drowning after more than 65 men in the last five years have been found dead in the canals and ponds of the Northern City of Manchester.

Talking to the broadsheet The Telegraph, he says, "The number is far higher than one would expect and from the data I just don't believe these were suicides; canals are not a popular site for suicide, and people rarely choose this for their method; but they make for ideal grounds for predators. Many of the reports from the coroners are inconclusive."

Professor Jackson, having accessed freedom of information reports regarding many of the deaths, has come to a grim conclusion. He doesn't believe they were accidents.

Pointedly he adds, "If you're trying to commit suicide by drowning, it's very hard to do in a canal- unless you can weigh yourself down with something heavy."

Some of the deaths it seems have clearly indicated that something else might be going on other than an innocent accidental fall into the canals.

He also points to the very clear victimology - they were all young males. He says there is a clear connection between the cases from the fact that the in at least 48 of the cases, the bodies were so badly decomposed as to be impossible to identify. This links them together connectively in his opinion.

If these victims were being randomly pushed in by someone vindictive, they would not all be successful attempts. At some point, one of the victims would fight, struggle, and not drown. People would soon hear about it. No-one has come forward to say this has happened to them, although doubtless the dark and dimly lit canals are excellent places for drug deals, and muggings.

If they were all cases of criminal attempts and 'success' by psychopathic muggers, why is it not happening in Cambridge, another University town with canals, or Universities by the sea, of which there are many, such as Bournemouth or Brighton?

Not only that, but with Newspaper reports carrying images of police teams being able to walk through some stretches of the canals because the water is not even knee deep, it does beg the question how could they all so easily drown in shallow water?

The canals of Manchester run through parts of the city centre, mainly the old industrial parts but also quite close to very busy nightclubs and bars. Manchester is both a thriving University town and has a popular Gay Village, and every night, bars are packed with drinkers.

Many will inevitably on occasion drink too much, some will as a result have accidents, however the canals are not obvious routes to take. They are not renovated scenic canals; rather they are dimly lit, strewn with litter and damp.

They aren't a short cut to anywhere and they aren't a route home. They're not somewhere anyone would go for a pleasant walk.

Yet some of the deaths have clearly indicated that something else might be going on other than an innocent accidental fall into the canals.

In the next case, a swear word uttered in what was both surprise and shock was the last thing his father heard, ending a fifty minute telephone call as his father kept him on the telephone, trying to find him.

His son had called him late that evening to say he'd run his car into a dried mud bank and couldn't get it out; it was stuck and he'd asked his parents to come and get him.

It was May 2008 and student Brandon had been driving home to Marshall in Minnesota; a rural and mainly agricultural county comprised mainly of canals and wind projects. In fact, he'd just completed a technical college course in wind turbines.

After waiting for a while for his parents to turn up he became impatient when they told him on the phone that they were having trouble locating him. He told them he was going to walk toward the nearest town, whose lights he said were in the distance and said that he expected them to meet him enroute.

However, it would seem that perhaps Brandon was slightly off in his description of where he thought he was, because no matter how hard his parents looked for him, they couldn't locate him or his car.

He continued walking on toward the lights in the distance as his parents searched for him, now well after midnight, and they stayed in contact throughout, with his Father keeping him talking on the telephone.

Brandon was certain he knew where he was and he couldn't understand why his parents couldn't find him and he was becoming increasingly irritated; yet his parents had gone to exactly where he said he was and he was definitely not there. They continued to drive around the roads, unable to see him or his car, and then came the swear word in which he sounded suddenly surprised and shocked, and the phone cut off.

It didn't sound like he had fallen over or tripped up; it sounded like he was shocked by something, even horrified by something; but by what?

Whatever it was, Brandon did not answer his telephone again, despite his father constantly calling his number back. Now his parents were concerned. He wasn't answering his phone for some reason and they had no idea what had just happened to him, where he was, or what might be happening to him still.

Desperately they continued to drive around, urgently trying to find his location, and get him to answer his phone, and in fact they proceeded to spend several hours that early morning desperately looking for him, yet still they failed to spot any sign of him.

Around dawn they called the police and a search for the missing student was immediately initiated. It wasn't until the following day that the police were able to locate his missing car, by tracing signals received at cell phone towers from his cell phone.

The car was in fact nearly twenty miles from the town the boy had thought he'd been heading toward on foot. He'd told his parents that he was close to the town when he'd called them to come get him. That was why they couldn't find him that night. He'd been nearly twenty miles away from where he thought he was. He'd thought that the lights he could see on the horizon were the town but he was wrong, he was many miles from the town, and so while his parents had gone to that location, he had been wandering around miles away from them.

That explained why they couldn't find him, but it didn't explain why he could not be found now. The search party could not find him, or his cell phone.

What investigators started to believe was that he'd accidently walked into and then fallen into the river as he was talking to his father. That could explain his shock, they thought.

His father wasn't convinced. He said he may have had a drink, and according to the friends he'd been with that evening, he had been drinking but definitely not enough for him to have been drunk, and his father said he didn't sound drunk throughout the phone conversation that lasted almost an hour. It didn't seem plausible that he could fall in and not get out.

Despite an exhaustive search of both the water and the land however, he could not be found. Searchers said the river was flowing fast at the time and could have swept him away, but the water was extensively searched and they could not find his body.

The searches included aerial searches, horseback, ATV and many friends and volunteers on foot. They looked repeatedly over the ground. After the official searches ended, his family, along with volunteers didn't give up however, and continued to look for him for weeks.

The only clue came from the K9 search dogs that seemed to indicate that his scent had travelled in one particular direction, but that did not lead to finding his body as the scent stopped. However perhaps that was a clue that he couldn't have gone in the water after all.

What did hamper the search efforts, particularly the ability to track his scent, is that the area by its geographical nature is one of criss-crossing winds that break up the flow of scent.

It was possible that he'd succumbed to hypothermia, especially if he'd walked through wet grass and been out in the cold for hours, but it was May, not winter, and even so, they still should have been able to find his body.

Did his call, which ended so abruptly in shock, indicate that he had somehow become the victim of foul play? Had someone arrived there at the scene? Had they abducted him? Was that why his body was never found?

His heartbroken mother talked to news channels after the incident. "He wasn't injured. He said he was ok, no damage to his car. He felt confident about where he was and he was saying that we were lost.

The minute the call dropped I became sick. I knew; I knew it was wrong and I knew it was bad."

Brandon Swanson is still missing.

Another man named Brandon, is Brandon Lawson, a 27 year old male who made a desperate call to 911 for help.

He was just off the highway outside of Bronte, Texas, when he called the police. It was August 2013 and just after midnight. He'd gone out for a drive to get some air, leaving his wife and children at home. Shortly after, he ran out of gas and he phoned his brother to ask him to come and help him.

While awaiting the arrival of his brother however, something happened that's hard to understand. He called 911, in some kind of trouble.

He tells them he's run out of gas and that he's in the woods just off the highway. It's hard to understand his exact words in the 911 call, but many who have heard it believe it's something along these lines;

"I got chased into the woods," or "There's guys chasing me in the woods."

He continues saying something that sounds like;

"Pushed some guy over. I accidently ran into them. I'm not speaking to them. I'm in the middle of a field. I ran into somebody. There is one car here. Got taken through the woods. Please hurry, please help."

He mentions other cars, other people, but again it's very hard to decipher although it's still on YouTube to listen to. Who were the other guys? What was going on?

That night, there was a lot of confusion. The police didn't turn up despite him saying he needed the police, not an ambulance, and asking them to "Please hurry."

A state trooper did arrive at the truck by chance, when he was driving by and saw it abandoned on the highway, but this was unrelated to the 911 call. His brother and his wife also arrived on the scene with a gas can.

The man in trouble called his brother while they were standing with the Trooper, but the signal was really bad and his brother could barely hear what was being said. He did hear the words, "I'm in a field," and that he said he was bleeding, but he automatically assumed that his brother was hiding out from the police because he'd just learnt he had an outstanding minor warrant.

Neither his brother and wife, nor the Trooper were aware of his call for help to the 911 dispatchers.

Obviously now in hindsight his brother realises that he was asking for help and was in trouble, but he didn't hear him properly at the time.

Since then there has been no sign of him. He has not been seen since.

The next day his family and the state troopers began searching for him when it was understood that he hadn't returned home.

An aerial search with infrared and a grid foot search were carried out. Later, cadaver dogs were brought in, but nothing was found of the man. Texas SAR did thorough and extensive searches in the area looking for any sign of him, in case he had got lost and lay injured, or had died out there.

According to his wife however, his last cell phone ping was received three miles from the area, and perhaps outside of the area at first searched. However, he still has not been found. No body, no clothes, no car keys or wallet; no trace of him.

His disappearance is truly a mystery, as is who was with him and possibly chasing him that night. He said in the 911 call that he was being chased by men in the woods. Who were the men and why were they chasing him?

When the Trooper and his brother arrived at his truck there were no other cars or trucks pulled over beside his. His own truck showed no signs of a collision or accident, so when he said he "ran into them," he didn't mean that he had an accident while in the car.

What does seem likely is that if he called 911 for help, he wasn't in fact hiding from the Cops in the woods. He'd called them himself asking for help.

Where did the car go that he said was near him when he called 911? Where did the men go? Why were they chasing him? What did they do to him? If he was bleeding, as he told his brother, why did the search dogs not pick up on his blood scent?

What happened out there in the dark that night?

His disappearance remains a complex and disturbing mystery, and his family have reportedly spent all of their savings trying to find him.

WISC-TV Madison Chanel 3000 reported on the disappearance of 22-year-old Josh Snell who vanished in June, 2005 in Eau Claire. His brother told reporters he had been in town to attend a wedding and that afterward, his brother had gone with friends to some bars in town. Four days later his brother's body was pulled from the Chippewa River. His brother said he does not believe his brother 'just wandered into the water.'

He went missing on the same day as Todd Geib, and Josh's last contact seems to have been when he called a friend late that night with a disturbing message.

In a phone call with a friend, "he said he was scared, that he was hiding in some brush, that he was running from someone. He said he didn't know who it was, or how he was going to get away. He said he didn't do anything, but he was terrified and he was scared for his life," Jon Snell says.

Another source quotes, "He called a friend to say that he thought unknown people were following him and that he might be in trouble with the police." The Local police said they had no contact with Snell however.

Are these young men being hunted via their cell phones? Chosen somehow and tracked via the signals given out from their cell phones?

S. Ward's brother also died in mysterious and suspicious circumstances. "Walton was last seen alive at Landsharks Bar, Indianapolis, with a 'bouncer' at approximately 1:20-1:30 am on October 12, 2012. His last attempt to save his own life was at 1:30 am when he dialled 911 from his Phone for help. His killers interrupted his 911 call and murdered him...He knew he was going to be killed. His desperate call lasted for 1-second which was just enough to register to the nearest cell phone tower...but it wasn't not long enough to save his life."

"That was the last time we know him to be alive, until the Construction workers discovered his body on October 22, 2012, floating in the River a few blocks from the bar (less than a mile) 10 days after his desperate call to 911 on that night. His phone was found on the bank of the River behind a Restaurant. The police said he must have been 'drunk', 'fallen in' or 'gone swimming' in the dead of winter."

Interviewed by crime writer, Eponymous Rox of the Killing Killers Blog Spot, his mother said,

"Where he was found, the depth was two feet. He was going (to the Bar) to meet a young woman he'd been talking with on OkCupid.com dating website. She didn't show up. She said she was from Brownsburg, Indiana. He said that she was in college and planning to become a lawyer. One odd thing that he mentioned about her was that she told him she'd got a college scholarship for wrestling. Looking into this, I have not been able to find any school that has a women's wrestling program. The Indianapolis PD did not question her and still have not had their cyber unit complete that part of the investigation."

"He had met up with her in the week prior to the night (he disappeared) and said that she'd come to meet him with a few friends, to make it more of a laid-back group. They were not going on a dinner-type date, it was more of a casual situation where they could hang out and get to know each other. It seemed to make sense that she was probably being cautious, as a young woman meeting up with a man that she met online. That Friday night, I understood that he would be meeting her and her same friends he'd met the other night."

His mother's testimony would appear to offer a couple of very intriguing possibilities; while a glance at college scholarships offered for women at colleges shows there are some, the statistics given of the percentage of female high school Wrestlers who go on to compete in college is just 3%. That's a tiny number. In a post on IndianaMat.com, which is a place 'to give people involved with wrestling in the state of Indiana promotion,' there's a post which says, "I'm a coach for Brownsburg MS (the area which the girl online said she was in school) My 8th grader is looking for scholarship opportunities. I was wondering if you have any advice?" It would seem then that they are not easy to come by then perhaps?

It was an online correspondence initially between the girl wrestler and the victim, until they met in person. Was it really a woman he was talking to, or was it perhaps a man pretending to be a woman who had been corresponding with him, who had slipped up when he said he had a wrestling scholarship? Is this a vital clue of a 'group' involvement? If so; why? And if so, who is behind this group? It's extremely unlikely that a young group like this could be planning and carrying out nationwide abductions and murders, Remembering that sometimes young men have gone missing in different states in the same manner on the same night; were this group who showed up the first time to meet her son, somehow recruited to play a key role, possibly like some of the bouncers too?

His date and her friends never showed up. While he was seen in other bars in the street and on CCTV in the bars, and while he left alone, his father says to journalist Eponymous Rox, "I believe he was murdered on the basis of his 911 call being at 1:40 am, terminated within a second. He was in excellent physical condition, capable of getting out of three feet of water, and, he was visiting from California and was not familiar with the area and accessible paths to the canal." (In other words, his father means, why would he have gone down to the canal if he didn't even know it was there?)

His mother says, "My conclusion is someone, (probably more than one) was with him. It's very suspicious and illogical that a very healthy, strong, trained athlete 'fell' and drowned in three feet of water on his own."

The same family have also written an article on their website, dedicated to the mystery of their own son's death, with regards to another young man. "Coincidence?" they ask, of the circumstances surrounding the death of another boy, Joshua Swalls, (whose Toxicology reports later came back to show that he was not drunk nor under the influence of recreational drunks) when the 22 year old also vanished, not far from where their son did, and was subsequently found dead three weeks later in a retention pond that had already been searched by police divers after he went missing.

He disappeared three weeks after their son, and had vanished from outside of a friend's apartment, leaving his car keys, wallet and phone inside. Ward's family say, "So now there are 2 men that go missing within 3 weeks and 2 miles of each other and are later found dead in bodies of water. Obviously, the police have to consider the possibility that something is wrong here, right? Wrong. The police say again; a case of "drunk and fell in."

However, that night Josh had not had anything to drink before going to his friend's apartment. He stayed just over 35 minutes and did drink at his friends, but as the later autopsy shows, he didn't have enough alcohol in his system to be classified as drunk. The biggest problem his family see is how and why the young man managed to get to where he did.

Ward's family too say, "To get into that pond, he would have to scale a 6 foot fence. How then, after he had enough coordination and presence of mind to figure out how to get into that pond, did he become so incapacitated that he didn't realize he was walking into freezing water and suddenly forgot how to swim? Does this not sound crazy to anyone else?"

In 2011, Mike Shaw wrote of the grief, anger and sense of helplessness that he felt because he could not save his best friend. "Sly McCurry did not walk out onto the ice of Lake Superior (Wisconsin) that cold January (2010) winter night and fall through and drown. He was murdered. No one can ever convince me it was anything but murder. He would never have went from the Nightclub to that secluded area alone in 20 degrees below weather, with no coat, and drown. He had no car and after being thrown out of the club via the back door, on the alleged grounds that he was drunk, he was left in the alleyway."

Crucially, he adds that his best friend was not very likely to have decided to 'go for a swim,' not only because it was the middle of winter, but also because he had cut a finger the same day while at work as a junior chef. His finger was in a bandage and had a splint on it.

Tracker dogs traced his scent at an exit door of the hotel he was staying in but it led no-where after that. This was done two days after he disappeared.

Late in May, four months later, his body was found in the lake. Mike points out, "His hotel was two blocks from the club; his body was found in the Tower Bay slip, nine blocks in the opposite direction."

Clearly then, the overt implication again is that he did not voluntarily go to that destination.

Says Mike, "Like clockwork, I see this killer(s) strike all over the North-eastern United States."

There are so many cases that have been mentioned in my previous books and that could be covered in this book; and they continue to happen, and the links to all the cases seem to be that the victims are separated from their friends, and often make a distressed telephone call.

What are the young men seeing moments before their phone calls get cut off? Who is taking them? And why?

What is happening? Is some kind of elite group conducting ancient alchemical rituals to further enhance their desire for dark power? It's not beyond the realms of possibility, and we don't have to believe in this arcane power; it's whether others believe in it that matters.

There are also recorded cases of a catholic college harbouring convicted sex molesters within their own clergy in one part of the country where a disproportionately high number of cases have happened, and allegations that two boy's scents led to the doors of the college, despite one of the victim's not having been in the area at all before disappearing.

However, this doesn't cover all the other cases statewide and possibly internationally.

On the other hand, as Professor Gilbertson and the detectives feel, this is a more organised form of 'terrorism,' by some kind of group intent on sending a message. What exactly that message is, who the group are, and why this specific victim-type is selected no-one knows.

The likelihood is that it's not 'serial killers' in the most commonly understood meaning of the term, but rather, something more sinister, more organised, and perhaps at a much higher level. Again, if it were serial killers, they would need to be able to be in more than one location at the same time, as sometimes incidents occur in separate states on the same night. There have been suggestions that it has something to do with College fraternities; but the deaths take place nationwide. On the other hand, it would be possible to co-ordinate.

Are the bouncers or bar staff, nearby construction workers, or cab drivers involved? Some think the police are complicit or directly involved. Theories from speculators across internet platforms over the years, on social media and in articles, are wide and ranging, and perhaps it's all hysteria; but the families and the previously mentioned experts don't think it is. They think there are far too many commonalities.

There are elements in the cases which could lead to a conspiracy theory that it's organised by an MK Ultra-style project and that the killers are doing this under instruction, as part of either their initiation or on-going training as 'assassins' for their masters, who are well hidden behind the smoke and mirrors. Researchers such as David McGowan and his book 'Programmed to Kill,' clearly provided allegations of possible serial killer assasins who have been created, manipulated and programmed long before now.

On the other hand, a cursory glance on forums that talk about these drowning deaths will show that there are many who look into the numerology aspects of it, or the names of the victims. They indicate and attempt to prove for example, that these victims are chosen and that a combination of the letters in their names and the places they are either taken from or found in, often spell out very intricate messages from the killers, drawn from ancient texts, movies, art and literature. The suggested clues are complex and would require months and months of analysis to verify if there really is anything to this idea. Is it a possibility? Certainly, but it's hard to prove.

If that were to be proven however, it would indicate that the killers are both highly educated and very intelligent. Some have posited that the killers are therefore from an elite 'hunting' group; from elite secret societies along the lines of such groups as 'the skull and bones' or a sub-strata of the illuminati.

As just one example, in a wordpress blog no longer available, but quoted in various forums, 'someone' has pointed out that the word NEMEC can be found from the first letters of the location in which several victims were found;

New London, Daniel Newville, (August 2002)

Eau Claire, Craig Burrows, (September 2002)

Minneapolis, Chris Jenkins, (October 2002)

Eau Claire, Michael Noll, (November 2002)

Collegeville, Josh Guimond, (November 2002)

Why is this possibly relevant? Well, in their opinion, this could apply to the name of an actor, Colin Nemec. He played the role of the true story of a boy called Steven Stayner. Coincidently, he was mentioned in my 'Mysterious things in the Woods' book, for the reason that after he was abducted as a child, his brother turned into a serial killer, who hunted, abducted and killed women in the Yosemite national park. In 1999, three female tourists had vanished from their rooms at the Cedar Lodge while in the park on a hiking trip. A few months later, they were found, brutally murdered in the woods.

Five months later, Joie Armstrong, 26, a naturalist at the Yosemite Institute, also went missing. Her truck was still parked in the driveway of her home at her cabin. Her body was found in the woods, not far from the cabin.

A park employee had noticed a car parked near her cabin on the night of her disappearance, and police issued an alert for the car. A few days later, police spotted the car parked up near Merced River Canyon. They came across a man wandering naked. He said his name was Cary Stayner and that he worked as a handyman at Cedar Lodge. After the encounter, investigators compared the car tyres to tyre tracks found at the crime scene, and they matched. The police found Stayner and arrested him. He confessed quickly and readily to all of the killings.

His own family history astonishingly revealed a disturbing crime perpetrated against his younger brother, and perhaps was what shaped him into becoming a serial killer.

At the age of seven, his brother had disappeared without trace one afternoon in 1972, while walking home from school alone along the Yosemite Highway. Eight years later, Cary had heard an announcement on the radio that his brother had been found. It turned out that his brother had been abducted by a paedophile and former employee of the Yosemite Lodge, and kept prisoner for all of those years. Investigators wondered if Cary's homicidal behaviour had been caused perhaps by his own family's experience.

Colin Nemec played the role of the young brother in the subsequent movie. Nemec talks about Cary Stayner in the book The Yosemite Murders. Nemec is also mentioned in the book *I Know My First Name Is Steven*, which talks about the abduction.

In the case of the person who posted this NEMEC theory, they link it to the ATWA movement of Charles Manson, with ATWA being the acronym he created standing for Air, Trees, Water, Animals and All the Way Alive; an ecological term the group designated to identify 'the forces of life which hold the balance of the earth.' With his small group of followers, prior to being imprisoned, it was Manson's attempt at eco living, though others say it was survivalist living.

In this case, the poster's theory, explained on themanyfacesofthezodiac.com/2013/04/07/charles-manson-link-to-smiley-face-murders/ follows through with the belief that the college killings are a continuation of the Manson group, and that they are examples of mind-controlled, programmed individuals. "The Manson Family through ATWA has grown to a point now where I am sure even the FBI does not know the number."

His implication is that the group never went away with Manson's imprisonment; it carried on.

Interestingly, this does tie in with David McGowan's position and his alleged research findings. He says that Mason's house was at one point in the same neighbourhood as Boy's Town, which was identified as an underground paedophile abduction ring during the Franklin Scandal (as referenced in 'Taken in the Woods' with regard to the Johnny Gosh abduction case). According to McGowan, researcher Joel Norris makes the allegation that Manson was involved in a murder for hire ring and child pornography. He also alleges that he uncovered his association with a satanic cult involved in sacrifice and murder. McGowan also states that another researcher, Ed Sanders, on interviewing Manson's associates, alleges that he was involved in the production of snuff movies. The theories go further, claiming that Manson was allegedly mind-controlled by the CIA through the use of drugs and programming, but it's not for this book to go that deep into things related to this and go way off topic. However, the idea is that this 'group' are in fact 'mind controlled assassins' who hunt the selected targeted male college victims.

Is any of this at all in any way relevant? Or is it all just insane ramblings and attempts to form theories from random coincidences found in words and letters?

According to the person who found this connection, their belief is "'NEMEC' was being formed at the exact same time he (Stayner) was on trial for murder and making big headlines in the newspapers." In other words, it was pre-determined and being carried out now, if not much before these drowning cases came to be noticed. The chances are then, they go back a lot more than a few years.

Is this delusional? Or is it an example of what this alleged unknown organised group of killers could be, and their sending out a message, 'hidden in plain sight? Is this all an absurd over-stretch to even try to see connections where there may be none? Very possibly, and patterns can be found anywhere if you look hard enough among the statistics. Statistics can be manipulated to back up findings. Micro-patterns appear that can be misleading when viewed as a whole.

That is just one of the theories however, for what it is worth; but there are many more, such is the mystery of these drowning deaths. They could be entirely misleading, or they really could be a sign, a message, hidden in plain sight, as per the methods used by such enigmatic and elusive groups as the supposed illuminati or lower echelons of.

Could it be part of an ongoing MK Ultra? When investigated, the program had consisted of 149 'subprojects' which the Agency had contracted out to various *Universities* and institutions. Is it still going strong?

Is it some kind of water boarding hazing initiation? Which goes too far, deliberately, to implicate those involved and serving as a perfect blackmail tool to use to keep them in the 'frat' or secret society for life?

The theories go on and on, and could fill numerous books and still be complete nonsense, although they do show how many people are so convinced that something sinister is indeed going on that they are prepared to dedicate extensive amounts of time trying to solve it. Sadly for now however, there is no clear answer. Or is it just simply misadventure and drowning? That is for the reader to decide.

Why are there no unsuccessful attempts? Why are there never any witnesses? Or are there?

Worryingly, no-one has ever yet seen them being abducted, and there are never any witnesses to the crime. Or are there?

One possible 'witness' has written to killing killers website, "I didn't make much of it at the time and didn't still until I moved to Minnesota and met a friend of one of the victims. When I was in college, in October 2000 I was found blacked out and vomiting. My memory is hazy but I'd met this guy who wanted me to follow him to another party. We walked on for several blocks and I kept asking where we were going. At first I was expecting the TKE house (Tau Kappa Epsilon Fraternity) but he said no. I asked if he was on the football team and he said no. He wouldn't tell me our destination. After a few more blocks I said I'd had enough and went home. In retrospect, where we were walking was toward the river that cut across campus, before I'd left him and gone... Made me scratch my head a little.'

Again, is his story true, or accurate? Although why would he make it up? There are other similar posts about men who say they have been separated by a group of both young men and women who they have met in bars. One of them talks about thinking something had been slipped into his drink and then resisted being pushed inside a van while walking along the street afterward. Another describes a man following him and then a van driving up fast and blocking his exit. There are numerous potential stories like this if they are looked for hard enough. Are these people just jumping on the bandwagon? Are any of these accounts true? Possibly they are.

Another weird account reads as follows, from a while before the current killings started, implying they could have been occurring a lot longer than perhaps realised.

"I attended high school in 1960, 1961 and 1962 in New York City. I have a strange story. A school mate Michael who I had lunch with is what this story is about..

Some things I definitely remember but generally some facts are vague to me. I definitely remember standing in front of the academic building at lunch time and speaking to Michael.

He said he had a boat and wanted me to go for a boat ride with him. (He may have indicated he had some friend that would also be there). He and his friends..

I believe prior to this meeting he had asked me what religion I was and I said Jewish.

I believe he confirmed this (insistently) once or twice.. At some point I believe he asked me if I could swim, also was I good swimmer..I would have said yes a good swimmer.

Michael then asked me to meet them in a specific location by the water in Brooklyn or Queens (one or the other).He said you know where that is and how to get there, I said no.. Then he asked about one or two more locations. I said no; he said take this train and that train; I said no, I am from the Bronx and I would get lost. Well he asked me, do I know any desolate area in Brooklyn or Queens? I said no. How about the Bronx? I said yes City Island, Orchard Beach.

He thought about it but said he wouldn't know how to get home from there.

Here is where the story gets strange. Michael says to me "never mind, there's no boat," ... "we were going to lure you there and kill you! You are going to get me in a lot of trouble with my family" he said! "I was supposed to bring you there and kill you and now I am in trouble with my family." I was still trying to have lunch with him as he walked away mad at me because he was now going to get in trouble for not bringing the (prey) to the water edge!!!! and don't I understand. At the time other than losing a friend (lunch buddy) this immediately rolled of my back like water on a ducks back and I did not think about it (or talk about it) for over 50 years...until now."

His story doesn't make a lot of sense in terms of the victims now and why such a group, if it existed, would be hunting and killing them as prey; but then it doesn't have to make sense to us; just them.

'TheyDontSee' posted on a facebook interest group,

"It's a group, both men and women, and government involved. It's co-ordinated. Victims aren't snatched; they're tricked then forcibly pulled into a van and subdued. It's serious (spiritual/occult) yet it's a game too. They use the internet to communicate but not 'publicly' on it. They're kept alive and groomed; brainwashing, mental torture, (not physically). They have existed for decades. On the east it's killing with a gun, then they decided it was 'safer' to do it this way and they're right; we're still looking for them.."

Is this from an insider into some of the investigations? Or, just a guess? Of course, there's every chance that some of the messages and opinions posted on the internet are from those within the groups itself. They are probably monitoring and reading it all.

Tomich Carpenter started a spreadsheet, gathering data to analyze for possible patterns. He believes he has found several similarities between the drowned men. 'I believe these students attended 'public' seminars and anyone interested were asked to stay after the meeting to learn more. That is where the recruitment started. Later people turned up drowned to scare those already indoctrinated to remain in.' It's a good theory. (Or, alternately perhaps, those who wanted no part of it but now knew too much about the existence of this recruiting 'group' were the ones killed-off.) 'These young men would fit into any community they were assigned to, to await further instruction. Money could be enticement' (or perhaps, status and recognition of their abilities as scholars and sportsmen initially could have been the hook that attracted them) 'and death could be punishment. Those that did not turn up drowned are living in other communities with new identities. This is a national security issue and I believe black ops is involved.'

Well, again, it's not beyond the realms of possibility. The deaths and the subsequent theories will continue until something is done to stop them.

Another post from a recent graduate of engineering, writes, "I live in Wisconsin. The night I'm about to describe has nagged at me for almost two years now.. I tried to ignore it but as one who always trusts my gut..

While still in school I was at a bar one night not far from the house I was living in at the time. I used to like to go the bar and do my homework. I know this sounds odd but I can tune out my surroundings.

I always sat at one end of the bar and worked on advanced math. This night I could feel someone's eyes, and looking up I saw a man sitting across from me. He was dressed very nice. We made eye contact and shivers went down my spine, but I went back to my work.

A few minutes later I felt alarmed, as unbeknown to me the man had came and was sat right next to me. (There were other empty seats along the bar.) He attempted small talk. I told him I was in engineering school. This really got his interest, and he kept asking more and more questions. He seemed very impressed that I held a 3.5 GPA again it really aroused his interest. I presumed he must be gay and trying to hit on me. I answered his questions bluntly, trying to end the conversation. It did not end. He kept trying to make talk and buy me drinks. After I kept refusing my guard really started to go up. He'd told me he wasn't from round here but travelled through for business; then his story changed to having friends close-by and did I want to go to there and smoke pot with him. I did smoke pot; but I hadn't told him that and he looked real square. All my radars were going off.

Eventually, I went to the bathroom and slipped out the back door. A few months later I stumbled upon the murder theories and chills went down my spine. After much consideration I contacted the investigators and told them. I said I could give a good description for a police sketch, but nothing happened and they never contacted me again.

The guy was creepy on so many different levels...and on a side note, the bar is just down from a secluded park by the river....'

Another lead or just another strange story? Who was the smartly dressed man; and were there more like him waiting outside somewhere in the darkness?

Chapter 9:
Shape-Shifters & Missing Time

It's a chilling tale of abductions, mutilations, murders of adults and children, time slips and sorcery, and it ended in 'the world's last witch-trial.' It took place in 1880 on a remote Chilean island called Chiloe and was said to have been carried out in the name of 'La Provincia Recta', translated as the 'Righteous Province.' This was the term given to the rulers there; a sect of warlocks who lived in a hidden cavern.

Gruesomely, these warlocks were said to take to the sky and fly around the Island wearing magickal 'clothing' which was made from the flayed skin of their deceased victims.

Lying close to the 35th parallel, the island has a mysterious and sinister history. It was the spot in which at the beginning of the 16th century the Inca Empire ended, and according to the Smithsonian, 'a strange and unknown world began.'

A place of rain and cold and untamed forests, to the Incas, it was a place where the Warlocks lived and evil came from. English travel writer Bruce Chatwin unveiled the history of the Warlocks to the world, describing them as male witches, "who existed for the sole purpose of hunting people."

According to their own testimonies at their trial, they ran protection rackets on the island, and would dispose of their enemies by sajaduras: that is, by magically inflicting cuts to the flesh.

Their headquarters was located in a cave, the entrance of which had been camouflaged to maintain its secret existence. It was lit with torches fuelled by the burning of fat from their victims' bodies. The warlocks and other witnesses swore at the trial that the cave was guarded by two monsters who ensured that no-one could enter and seize the secret treasures they kept there, including an ancient leather spell-book and a bowl, which when filled with water was said to allow secrets to be seen in it.

Mateo Coñuecar was one of the Warlocks who gave testimony, and he described his first time visiting the secret cave when he was a young initiate.

He said that he had been ordered to go to the cave to feed the 'creatures' inside of it. He went with another Warlock, who, when they approached the destination of the cave, began to dance ritualistically in order to open the cave entrance. He used a "special alchemy key," to open it, and the layer of earth hiding it came away.

Two disfigured entities burst out of the darkness at them. One he described as looking like a 'goat, which dragged itself on four legs.' The other was a naked man. The man was an 'invunche;' a deformed man who had been abducted as a baby and taken to the cave to become its guardian.

After being taken from its home and brought to the cave, according to Chatwin, its arms, legs, hands and feet were purposely dislocated. Then the warlocks got to work on its head. This was a slow and methodical task whereby each day, the baby's head was twisted a tiny fraction more than the day before so that eventually it was rotated by a full 180 degree and the child could look straight down the line of its own spine.

Chatwin continues, "Once the child is able to do this, the final adaptation is done. On the night of a full moon, the child is laid prostrate and tied down and its head covered over. A 'specialist' then takes a sharp knife and cuts a deep hole under the right shoulder blade. Into this hole he places the child's right arm and then sows up the hole. The child has now become the cave guardian; the 'invunche.'

It is kept in the cave forever and fed with human flesh. It never learns to speak nor read or write. It responds only with guttural noises.

The tiny populace of the Island were terrified of the Warlocks and their supernatural powers. The Warlocks claimed they would fly at night, in the human skin they wore which glowed with shiny phosphorescence from the grease of the skin. They claimed they could turn themselves into any animal, being 'Shape-shifters.' They could magically transport themselves to a 'Caleuche,' a ghost ship. It was a glowing ship that today is still seen by islanders. Many of them believe that the ship is a harvester of souls.

In order to become one of the Warlocks, an initiate must wash away their sins in the freezing sea for night after night and then prove they are cleansed of all human emotions and feelings by killing a member of their own family.

It was claimed that once they had passed their initiation, the secret sect would then celebrate their new member joining, by feasting on the roasted flesh of a new-born.

According to the warlock named earlier, he carried out 'hits' for payment. When a woman on the island went to him because her husband had been seduced by another woman, he killed the love rival for payment of not money, but cloth.

Since the times of the witch trials, Chiloe has lost none of its mystery. It's said to be a place where it's almost as though a parallel universe exists with it or alongside it, for there have been many unexplained disappearances and bizarre events. Steeped in mythology and folklore, there have been sightings of a variety of odd creatures, including the 'brujos;' shape-shifters who are immortal and who can take the form of wolves, fish, or humans. They can even take the form of rocks. It has been said that when they take the form of a human they are always very tall, and blonde. Sightings of these beings go back to before the time of Columbus yet there were no Caucasian blond races in South America before Christopher Columbus. It's these Nordic looking human's who are said by the inhabitants to be behind the disappearances of people on the Island.

Along with the Nordic sightings are the reports of the Ghost ship, the Caleuche, which again is reported to be able to shape-shift. When described, it bears striking similarities to UFO sightings in terms of appearance, and those who have seen it have also often reported incidents of missing time and relocation from where they last were. Some have described it as without doubt a ship, while others have said it has glowing lights, and yet other witnesses talk of strange glowing rocks or trees. Along with the sightings are usually the simultaneous reports of the most beautiful and ethereal sound of music. Those who have the sighting are often abducted; those who do not see it but hear the music have been reported to have become deranged as a result.

The Chilean newspapers have reported on cases of young men who have disappeared as youths, never to be seen again until decades later when they have reappeared as old men. One such case was reported by the journalist Antonio Cardenas Tabies, who spent many years obsessed by the strange accounts he kept hearing. In his book, 'Boarding the Caleuche,' he collected more than 50 testimonies of local islanders in the 1970's; all of varying ages and backgrounds. One man he interviewed as a boy of 16 had gone fishing alone one day when he suddenly disappeared. Two days later he was found alone and wandering aimlessly along the beach on the Island. He seemed to be in a complete daze when he was found, and when he was asked where he'd been, he said that when he got to a small hill that overlooked the ocean he began to hear a strange hum, like the sound of a generator running; but he said it was more like two generators running together at the same time. That was the last thing he could remember until he was found on the beach two days later. When he was taken back to his home, his family were very concerned when they saw that under his shirt he had a large scar that he had not had before. It was a huge scar that was shaped like a hand with long thin fingers.

When they asked him how he had got it, he could not remember and he said that he didn't recall having been in any pain. Even stranger, the scar looked like it had been there a long time, not like it was a fresh wound. Antonio Tabies returned to interview the same man five decades later, when he was by then in his sixties. The grown man was reluctant to be interviewed again, and when asked about the scar he said that he could not reveal how he had got it or he would die.

The reason for Antonio's own obsession with interviewing people was that he too had a similar inexplicable incident when he was growing up, of missing time and then being 'returned' to the Island changed.

Conclusion

Sometimes predators are animal or human....*and sometimes they are not.*

Excerpts from Mysterious things in the Woods

Introduction

Mysterious deaths in a forest said to be controlled by Satanists; Mountain climbers found inexplicably mutilated; large numbers of college aged men found dead in creeks; a hiker walks over the top of a hill in front of the rest of the hiking party and has vanished by the time they crest the hill, moments later; the little boy who says he was taken by a 'shimmering woman' in the forest; the village of native Inuits that 'disappeared'; a child playing near their parents in a forest, disappears in the blink of an eye without making a sound; hunters found dead in strange circumstances; experienced climbers disappearing, their bodies never found; missing bodies found, placed as though deliberately intended to be found.

No screams for help, no signs of the missing person; vanished into thin air. No trails or tracks left, no clothing found, no smoke, no shelters, no clues...

One only need search the internet briefly to come across the many disturbing cases of missing persons in rural areas that have been covered by both local and national newspapers for *decades*.

These and many other mysterious incidents in rural locations in America, Canada, Australia, England and indeed worldwide, have sparked debate by many into what could possibly be the cause.

There are many theories....and with these theories comes the visceral, primal fear that comes from the thought that we humans may be victim to a predator, that in the blink of an eye, outsmarts us very easily. Stalked as prey and snatched without warning... Never to be seen again. Or found, in the most horrible of circumstances....

Chapter One:
The Clapham Wood Mystery.

The 'Clapham Wood Mystery' refers to the woodland area, in West Sussex, England, where many believe satanic and alien activity has long been an occurrence, causing the deaths of pets, and even people.

The area is allegedly imbued with an eerie atmosphere, which can make those who visit it feel very unwell.

Fortean Times Magazine covered the story of how, since the 1960's, there have been reports of UFO sightings, and sensations of being physically attacked while in the woods, as well as a number of mysterious fatalities.

Reports exist from those who claim to have felt suddenly nauseous upon being in the forest; of being followed by someone or *something* unknown, and of being physically attacked by something, whilst others say their dogs have gone missing while out on walks there.

Policeman Peter Goldsmith's body was found hidden amongst the trees in 1972; a Vicar was found dead after disappearing in the forest; then, the body of Jill Matthews was discovered horribly murdered in 1981.

Paranormal and occult investigators Charles Walker and Toyne Newton detailed their own investigation of the place in a 1987 book, after they had carried out a comprehensive investigation into the believed use of the woods by a satanic cult, which they claimed was named 'Hecate,' after the goddess of magic and witchcraft.

Charles Walker has been quoted as stating that when investigating the strange area, he appealed for information from local people and met with a man in the woods, who threatened serious repercussions should he continue his investigation, claiming the support of some very powerful connections who 'would tolerate no interference,' in their ritualistic slaughtering.

Walker says mysteriously, "The human disappearances, of which there were several, ended up as Open verdicts. Searches were made of the likely routes; paths these people were thought to have taken and nothing was found...then sometime later, bodies were found in areas known to have been extensively searched by the Police." In other words, it would seem that the bodies were kept, either alive or dead, for some time, prior to them being placed back at a spot where they were most likely to be discovered. Echoes of similarity are found in a number of mysterious disappearances in national parks in America and Canada, as well as in bodies of water across America, (more on which will be covered in the next two chapters on the Smiley Face killers, and Mysterious disappearances in National Parks.)

According to Toyne Newton, a skeptical investigator named Dave Stringer of *the Southern Paranormal Investigation Group*, visited the Clapham Woods with a Geiger counter in 1977, and it began to register at an alarmingly high level. Mr. Stringer stopped, looking around him with concern. He said that then, suddenly, he saw a dark shape about 12 feet tall, which he could only describe as a 'black mass.' Seconds later, he claimed a large white disk object shot out from the trees, disappearing fast into the sky. The dark mass subsequently then disappeared.

Extremely curious, Stinger allegedly retraced his last steps and found, at the spot where the form had manifested, an imprint of a four toed footprint.

Interestingly, several miles to the North of Clapham Woods, is Chanctonbury Ring, which is again thought to be the location of possible satanic worship. The infamous occultist Alistair Crowley believed it was a place of great dark power. Clapham Woods, Chanctonbury Ring and another nearby Iron Age hill fort known as Fissbury ring, are all said to be linked by a mystical triangle of Ley lines.

Chapter Two:
The Bennington Triangle

The 'Bennington Triangle' was named as such by a New England author Joseph A. Citro during a radio programme in 1992, a play perhaps on the name 'Bermuda triangle,' to describe an area of the South-western region of Vermont, where a number of people went missing between 1920 and 1950.

Bennington was a small town near the mysterious Glastenbury Mountain. European settlers who founded their homes there began to tell of seeing unusual lights over the mountain. Tales of hairy 'wild men,' and other strange bigfoot-type beasts in the woods abounded. The mystery deepened enormously however in 1945. Seventy-four year old Middie Rivers was familiar with the wilderness area. He was an experienced hunt and fishing guide. On November 12, 1945, he escorted a party of four hunters into the mountainous woodlands.

Leading the way back to their campsite, Rivers suddenly disappeared from view, and seemingly vanished, leaving only one clue. An extensive search was instigated, but investigators found only a single bullet beside a stream-bed. No trace of Rivers was ever found.

Middie Rivers disappearance was the first in a series of missing person's cases over the next five years. In December, 1946, a year later, Paula Weldon, a sophomore at Bennington College vanished while hiking along Glastenbury Mountain's 'Long Trail'. A couple who had been behind her told searchers that they had seen her turn a corner, but when they reached the corner, Paula was gone.

Although the search and rescue team called in the FBI, as they did in Middie Rivers' case, again, no trace of Paula Weldon was ever found.

On Columbus Day 1950, eight-year-old Paul Jepson disappeared from the family farm. No trace of the child or his bright red coat was ever found, although hundreds of volunteers combed the mountainside in search of him.

Then, just three weeks later, 53-year-old Frieda Langer slipped into a mountain stream while hiking with her cousin. Telling her cousin that she would catch up with him after changing into dry clothes, Frieda disappeared on the walk back to camp.

Subsequent search teams scoured the area on foot, and by helicopter, but found nothing. Another four more searches were then carried out, with more than 300 strong parties made up of the military, police, and volunteers, but all came up empty-handed. Then, in May, her body was discovered; in an open area where she could not have been missed during the search, in an area that had been thoroughly searched many times before in the attempts to find her.

Again, as in the Crawley Woods cases, there is the implication that her body was seemingly deliberately placed there to be found.

Oddly, the cause of her death was determined as 'unknown.' According to some sources, one witness stated that, the body appeared fresh; it was as though Freida had died only moments earlier, "like she had died of fright."

The implication here is obviously that her body, alive, had been kept somewhere by someone or 'something' in all of the months between her disappearance and her being found.

Rumours and theories abound about the location and the reason for people's fate in the mysterious location. Some believe a Bigfoot-like "Bennington Monster" is the perpetrator, others cite they are alien abductions, while others feel there is a portal in the area, which opens to another dimension. More believe it to have been a serial killer, while the more rational amongst speculators will say that accidents happen in such areas, due to the very nature of the great outdoors, and that in terms of numbers, this is a very tiny proportion of people, given the huge amount of visitors to national park and forest areas such as Bennington.

Can any of these answers explain why in Maddie's case, her body was found without any decomposition, or where she had indeed been in the forest for the several months before she was suddenly found dead? Or why she was returned to the area where she disappeared, as though placed there?

Excerpts from Predators in the Woods

Chapter Six.
Things with Wings

Caretaker Mr Marielli who lives in Oakland Creek, California, claimed he saw a very odd and terrifying sight one night back in October 1975.

He didn't speak out about it then; he was sure people would think him crazy if he did.

He recalls that as he took out the garbage that dark evening, something above him caught his eye.

"It was like some fearsome gargoyle, on the edge of the roof of the house."

It was staring down at him.

"It was very broad; much bigger than a man. It was monstrous. I was always afraid to tell anyone though; but it was like the devil himself."

What he didn't know at the time however, was that he wasn't the only one to encounter such a monstrous thing. Winged, gargoyle-like monsters were being seen in trees and on roof-tops throughout the area. They had massive wings, and seemed to glide silently without needing to flap their wings.

Unknown magazine, published from 1997 to early 2001, interviewed a group of youths about their strange encounter in an Illinois park. One of the boys, Ron Bogaski, told of how he and several other of his friends came face-to-face with a gargoyle.

The night it took place was in 1981, in a park on a late summer's night. They were sitting beside an old mausoleum inside the park, when suddenly they noticed an incredible sight. Sitting on the top of the gothic structure was a creature, estimated to be possibly ten feet in height, with dark leather-like skin covering it. Its body was 'very muscular with thick arms. It had enormous wings and horns on its head.'

All four of the teenagers could smell the stench of decay coming from it, along with an overpowering smell of sulphur. They watched in awe and horror as it unfurled its wings and flew up into the night sky.

~~~

Respected researcher Stan Gordon reports on the alleged sighting of a dragon-like creature seen flying in Pennsylvania, in 2012.

In a rural part of town, a man was out walking his dog at close to midnight. He heard a 'woosh,' and looked up at the night sky. Flying over him was a large thing approximately fifty feet above that looked like a mythical creature; "It looked like a dragon," the shocked man reported.

It flew over a light and the man was able to catch a better look at it. He described its body as being over twenty feet in length and with a wingspan almost as wide. It didn't have scales, but rather had a shiny, almost reflecting skin. It was coloured reddish-brown. He could see arms that were muscular and legs that were thick. Both its mouth and its eyes appeared to be glowing. The noise coming from it was deep and throaty.

~~~

On unexplained mysteries forum, a lady in her sixties now relates the experience she had as a teenager.

"In 1963, I was 15, and my younger sister and I lived in Colma, California. My Mom used to send us berry picking in a wild area nearby. That day, as we started collecting the berries, I looked down the hill next to us and saw a large dark object lying there.

I was curious and climbed down to it. There was this huge dead dragon-thing. It was about 8 feet long with huge wings and claws. It was stiff. It had long sharp teeth... It was grotesque. I screamed and my sister came running. We both ran home screaming.

Over the years I have found stories that say they are mythical; but I know what I saw and it was a real gargoyle. My sister and I both saw it."

Recent Gargoyles have been reported since 2010 in Puerto Rico, according to investigator Reinaldo Rios and the Guanica police.

Incredibly similar eyewitness reports describe demonic looking entities of reptilian appearance, at least 6 feet in length, with leathery wings and skin, and red or yellow eyes full of intensity and menace.

~~~

A few days before, and directly after the 9/11 terror attacks in New York, witnesses and images show a huge winged entity flying from the twin towers. It seemed that Mothman had re-appeared at a scene of devastation, as it had allegedly done before; showing up at the Chernobyl nuclear disaster, and indeed at Fukashima.

Eminent researcher Colin Andrews posted a reported sighting by English businessman David Haith, who had written to him to tell him of what he had seen in 2011; prior to the Fukashima disaster.

"I was in Japan for business and staying with a friend who was teaching there. After dinner, he said he needed to see a weather project the students had created, near a power site.

As we walked toward the small weather project, we heard a sound like a bus's brakes in need of service then a scream that made the hairs on the back of my neck stand.

A young couple nearby were staring at the power plant, and a figure was silhouetted there on top of one of the buildings. To say that this creature was large was an understatement.

Suddenly it unfurled a huge set of black wings and took flight, circling several times, its attention fixed on a building below; that I was to later find out were the nuclear reactors.

Then it came toward us. It had two large eyes, glowing blood red. It was looking straight at us, but it flew toward the town.

We went straight home. My friend was shaking as he bolted the door shut; he couldn't believe what we saw. Finally he convinced himself it had just been an optical illusion; until he saw the News and the Nuclear disaster was reported.'

~~~

There are other reports of a Mothman creature being seen at an area of swine flu outbreak. Engineer Fransisco Torres told *Inexplictica* investigators that people had been seeing a tall creature, over nine feet tall, with huge wings and red eyes in La Junta, Mexico.

One witness, a young student at the North Region University, who asked them for confidentiality, claims that the strange entity even chased him.

He said that he was driving home after class one evening when he saw something in the road ahead of him. It looked like a man, hunched over and wrapped in something. Then suddenly it stood, and taking two steps it opened a huge pair of wings and flew toward the young man's car. It kept apace with the car as the student tried to drive faster to escape it until after several minutes of sheer panic, the enormous 'bird like' thing flew away.

~~~

In September 1978, workers arriving for their shift at a coal mine in Freiburg, Germany, saw a tall man standing in the opening of the mine, wearing a trench coat.

As several of the coalmen approached him to see he wanted, they were suddenly stunned to see a cape-like cloak unfurling around the man. Then they began to feel the most terrible horror as they realised it was no man standing there. As the 'cloak' unwrapped they realised it was a pair of huge wings, uncovering the body that was not human.

The scream it then emitted chilled their blood and hurt their ears.

Reports were that it sounded like fifty people screaming all at once; others said it was more like a train screeching on tracks as though the brakes had been applied in emergency.

Recoiling in utter fear and horror as it stood motionless in front of them, the miners retreated from it. They remained some distance away from it for a long time, until it disappeared inside the mine entrance.

Very reluctant to enter inside, the miners continued to stay out of the mine, until suddenly they were all thrown to the ground by a huge explosion coming from inside the shaft.

When the mine inspectors arrived to investigate the damage the explosion had caused inside, they were adamant that had the miners been inside at the time of the explosion, they would all have been killed.

Speculation rose that the creature, though terrifying in its appearance had come to warn them and to prevent them from going to their death. Others felt the creature had somehow purposely caused the explosion.

Excerpts from Something in the Woods is Taking People

Chapter Ten:
The Work of Satanists?

The Jamison family; husband, wife and their six year old daughter headed out to the Latimer Mountains of Oklahoma looking for a new home to move to, on October 8th 2009.

After their family realised they had not returned an enormous search party was organised with hundreds of volunteers, troopers from the Oklahoma Highway Patrol and agents from the FBI.

The searchers combed the area on foot, on ATV's and on horses but they found nothing; even with the sixteen teams of tracking dogs that had been used.

Then a few days later their truck was discovered by hunters. It was locked and inside it the family's dog was close to death. Investigators discovered the family's cell phones and a very large amount of cash. There were no tracks however to lead them to where the family could have gone.

The 31-year-old Sheriff, a former U.S. Army Ranger, said his mind was consumed by questions and theories.

"Throughout this whole process I've found myself going back and forth as to what might have happened," Israel Beauchamp said. "I'm at my wit's end. I asked for all the help I could get. FBI agents; private investigators who contacted me."

If it had been straight forward foul play, surely the perpetrators would have stolen the money; there was over $30,000 in cash in the vehicle.

A man who lived a quarter mile from where the pickup was found was the last known person to see them. He too was questioned. He saw no-one else in the vicinity.

Many have wondered were they drug users? Was it a drug deal gone bad? Others have wondered were they in the process of turning state's evidence against drug dealers?

Was it simply a criminal case, or was something much deeper to this?

As people in the area speculated and tried to understand what had happened to the family, an edition of *The Oklahoman* headlined the story. The mother of Sherilyn Jamison was telling the Newspaper that her daughter "was on a cult's hit list."

According to Oklahoma's *Red Dirt News*, husband Bobby had allegedly been reading a "Satanic Bible" and had asked a Church Minister how he could obtain "special bullets" that would enable him to kill the demons that were terrorizing the family.

Security camera footage recorded at their home, installed by the family due to their concerns of the alleged spiritual attacks they were complaining of. It shows both adults walking around at times in a trance-like states and disorientation prior to their departure.

Approximately a month before the disappearance of the family, local Pastor Carol Daniels was found horrifically murdered in her Church nearby. The local D.A. Mr Burns said of the crime scene that it was "the most horrific he'd ever seen," but he wouldn't go into details as to why. Her mutilated body though was found behind the Church Altar in a crucifix pose, obviously suggesting a link to Satanic ritual.

Then in November 2013 bodies of two adults and a child were found by a deer hunter about four miles from their truck. It was believed to be the skeletal remnants of the family.

This was odd because the Jamison father could not walk more than a few metres without experiencing severe pain, and Cherylin had chronic pain in her neck and shoulder. Both were on disability, yet they were found on the opposite side of the low mountain area where they'd left their truck.

Their 'abduction' has echoes of eerily similar unexplained missing person's cases that have been documented over the last couple of centuries; the 'abduction' takes place in a remote wilderness area with dense or difficult terrain.

The 'abductors' one assumes, must have had the ability to not only control and transport these people from their truck through rugged terrain; they also left no other vehicle tracks, nor footprints, nor scent.

While the Jamison's fate may simply be a case of human intervention, *Reddirt news* make a point of the synchronicity that both the area where their bodies were found, and the site of the Church where the pastor was murdered fall on the 'Occult line of tragedy;' on the 33rd parallel north.

Occultists see the number 33 as containing the highest of sacred power. Occult scholars and conspiracists claim that the Illuminati and the 'power elite' have staged murders on or near the 33rd parallel north throughout history.

In Occult belief, sacrificial rites enacted at the 33rd parallel have far more power than any other geographical locations. 33 is the satanic number of completion, and holds the power of transmutation.

According to expert Occultists and conspiracists alike, including the late occult researcher John

Downard, it's the 'kill number;' and the murders carried out are for a ritual called the 'Killing of the Kings' where the life-force is believed to be passed from the victim at the point of death to those carrying out the ritual.

They point to the grand events of the Hiroshima atom bomb, the JFK assassination, and the bombing of Babylon in the Iraq War, as all being planned along this sacred line.

Curiously, there was a similar case in 2013 in Eufaula, the Jamison's home town. Thirty year old Native American Tommy Eastep vanished on his return journey after spending a July 4th weekend trip there visiting his family. His truck was found abandoned on September 29th, in a rural area north of Holdenville; his keys, credit card and driver's license locked inside.

According to his older brother Clint, talking on blog talk radio, it was a good four miles off the main highway on a county road more like a cattle road. He says, "It was parked as deep as you could go. It probably stopped because there was overhanging tree and the truck couldn't go any further. There's a lake nearby, lots of small ponds around, and a large heavily-wooded area to the south and west.

Clint says, "He was a family man. He had kids. He wasn't in any type of turmoil, you know, that he walked off without his license, his debit card, his keys, his vehicle, and his belongings. He did not walk away."

Despite tracker dogs searching throughout the area his truck was found in, no trace of him has been found still. There is no suggestion here of occult intervention, although again his abandoned vehicle was found at a cross roads on the same symbolic degree of latitude.

Returning to the Jamison family, some sources including Discovery TV state that the tracker dogs *did* trace their scent, to a water tank near where their vehicle was found. This was an indication that their bodies had likely been placed inside the water tank, but when it was emptied they were not found.

Were they killed in the water? They were found almost three miles away with no tracks and both were partially disabled and unlikley to have walked that far voluntarily. Despite the search radius being extensive, they were not found during all the searches. Where had they been? Were they being kept somewhere? Were they kept in the water tower?

Adding to the water ritual theory is also the very odd case of Elisa Lam, whose death features a water tower; only in her case she was found dead in the water, unlike the Jamison family, who it can be suggested had been placed in the water and then removed.

This time the water tank was on the rooftop of a hotel. Partly captured on film is the shocking and mysterious death of Elisa Lam.

In June 2013, investigators ruled her death as 'accidental.' Several important questions however have failed to be answered. One of which is, why did she climb over fifteen feet up into a water tower on the roof of a hotel to get inside it? Another would be, what exactly was happening to her in the security footage of her in the hotel lift prior to her disappearance?

The twenty one year old Canadian student was staying at a cheap hotel in downtown Los Angeles while travelling on her own, taking some time out from college. She was found naked in the water tower, having been dead for two weeks. She was last seen on the CCTV camera in the lift, sometime before she ended up in the water tower. The parts in between are a mystery, but so too is what's happening to her in the lift.

Able to be watched on YouTube, the footage is difficult to comprehend and very eerie to watch. There is something very wrong going on.

She is seen entering the lift and pressing lots of the buttons quickly, then peeking out of the open door several times while she waits for the lift to close. It's almost as though she is fearful that someone is after her. Looking along the corridors, she waits as the lift door fail to close. Becoming increasingly distressed, she's seen making odd gestures with her hands, stepping out of the lift and hiding in the corridor, seeming to be terrified yet not fleeing the scene.

Is her imagination playing tricks with her? Is her killer there out of sight of the CCTV, but lurking within inches of her, waiting to abduct her? Is there something otherworldly about what is happening?

Some people studying the tape have implied there are strange shadows and movement seen inside the lift; shadowy movement, and even face-type forms appearing on the walls of the lift. Is this merely poor video quality and over-active imaginations, or was there something unidentifiable and supernatural manifesting in the lift with her?

At one point, she is seen waving her hands around in front of her, as though trying to feel for what is touching her and talking to her, that she cannot see. When she realises there is an intangible, invisible entity inside the lift with her, her horror grows and she becomes terrified, wrenching her hands together and bending her knees in fright, trying to maintain her grip on sanity when she does not understand what is happening to her.

Her behaviour is one of disorientation, fear, helplessness and shock. Some will say she was on drugs but none were found in her system. Others will say she was having a break-down but the tragic case has fascinated many and there are some incredible theories going around. Some strongly believe she was about to be attacked by something unseen.

Others feel her strange behaviour points to demonic possession and that she was clearly hearing voices. There's also the theory that she may have she died in an occult ritual; that she was used as a sacrifice, hinting at her name and the likeness to Aleister Crowley's poem 'Jephtha,' written when he was staying at the Cecil Hotel in London, the same name as the hotel in which she died.

They have pointed out that the poem has the line 'Be seen in some high lonely Tower.' In the poem, 'Jeptha' was a judge in the *Pseudo-Philo* works, (an ancient biblical text) who offered his daughter as a willing sacrifice. The girl is called Seila; an anagram of Elisa.

A coincidence perhaps? A conspiracy too far?

Others have speculated that she had been wanting to commit suicide. The hotel itself has an unsettling history of murder which may perhaps have left some kind of supernatural imprint on the building; its malevolent aura urging people on to commit acts of murder there. There are records of two serial killers having lived at the hotel. The hotel has also had an unusually high number of suicides.

However, there were far easier ways to do it. Was it even possible to get into the water tank of her own accord? There was no ladder there.

Is this all hysteria and speculation? Was she simply trying to get an old tempremental lift to move, by getting in and out of it and pressing all of the buttons, trying to see which one would get it moving?

But why does the security tape look like she's talking to someone who is not visible and reaching her hands out and grapsing the empty space in front of her as though trying to feel for something invisble that is right in front of her but that she cannot see. What is making her so distressed and confused?

Adding to the mystery is Dr Douglas James Cottrell, PhD. A highly regarded Canadian medical intuitive who claims he, like his predecessor Edgar Cayce, can access the Akashic Hall of Records. Through this he has given thousands of personal readings to people regarding their health problems, accessing their undiagnosed illnesses through a form of 'remote viewing.'

A former skeptic himself, it was when his child was born with a serious illness that he sought help with the diagnosis and through this journey met others like him who could help heal people. He undergoes deep meditative states to look into the past and the future, and is believed to be able to make accurate predictions and see what happened in past events. In one session available on YouTube, he relates what he 'sees' as having happened to Elisa Lam in the lift and up on the roof of the hotel.

He alleges that she was hearing voices in her head; but this was not from a psychotic breakdown, and it was not a demon. The voices were being 'beamed' into her head. They were calling her name, beckoning her; she was looking for the source of the voices and could not understand why she couldn't see the person or people around her when the voices were so close.

They were high pitched and uncomfortable, they were causing her distress, disorientation and fear. She was obeying the voices, going to where they were beckoning her so that she could find them. They led her to the water tower, says Dr Cottrell. They led her to her death and when she got to the roof he alleges, in his meditative trance state, there were pains in her head as though someone was pointing a laser beam at her head. Self-destructive thoughts were being given to her through the sound waves being sent through this 'laser' he claims.

Chillingly he says he can see a dark figure on the roof; cloaked in dark shiny clothing, a shadowed figure with its head covered by a balaclava or hood. He thinks it's a man but he also says it's possible it's a *discarnate* entity.

Others point to her online activity. Was a tweet allegedly sent from Elisa's twitter account really hers? There's the claim that from her twitter account, before her stay in the hotel, she tweeted a post about a Canadian company being given funding from the US for developing a 'quantum stealth' type of camouflage for soldiers that makes them invisible. The gear blends light around the wearer/ or an object, to create the illusion of invisibility. In that respect, a soldier, or anyone using it, can render themselves invisible to everyone else.

Has the development of cloaking technology created invisible predators that the unsuspecting person is powerless to see coming? Are people being silently snatched by something human but invisible?

These wild ideas and speculations could all be a range of conspiracy theories that have gone way too far, but perhaps not…….

End

The strange and mysterious disappearances and deaths just keep continuing. There is no one answer; only some very disturbing possibilities.

This is a puzzle. An often deadly one; but perhaps some of the possible perpetrators have now been identified.

Or perhaps the mystery remains, as one of the most enigmatic and perplexing of all time.

Contact details for Steph Young

Facebook StephYoungAuthor

Email StephenYoungauthor@hotmail.com

If you have experienced something strange and unusual like this, that's hard to explain, please feel free to let me know. I'm actively continuing to research and would be very interested.

Made in the USA
Middletown, DE
05 April 2016